How to Manage an Effective Nonprofit Organization

How to Manage an Effective Nonprofit Organization

From Writing and

Managing Grants to

Fundraising, Board Development,

and Strategic Planning

Michael A. Sand

CAREER
PRESS
Franklin Lakes, NJ

HOW TO MANAGE AN EFFECTIVE NONPROFIT ORGANIZATION
EDITED AND TYPESET BY
CHRISTOPHER CAROLEI
Cover design by Foster & Foster, Inc.
Printed in the U.S.A. by Book-mart Press

To order this title, please call toll-free 1-800-CAREER-1 (NJ and Canada: 201-848-0310) to order using VISA or MasterCard, or for further information on books from Career Press.

CAREER
PRESS

The Career Press, Inc., 3 Tice Road, PO Box 687,
Franklin Lakes, NJ 07417
www.careerpress.com

Library of Congress Cataloging-in-Publication Data
Sand, Michael A.
    How to manage an effective nonprofit organization : from
  writing and managing grants to fundraising, board development,
  and strategic planning / by Michael A. Sand.
       p. cm.
    Includes index.
    ISBN 1-56414-804-1 (pbk.)
    1. Nonprofit organizations—Management. I. Title.

HD62.6.S346 2005
658'.048--dc22

                                                2005046954

Dedication

This book and my life are dedicated to my wife and best friend, Diane. As I led workshops for nonprofit managers over the years, and provided on-site assistance to nonprofit agencies, I accumulated the tips included in this book. I want to thank all the individuals who choose to work in nonprofits, most of whom are overworked and underpaid. In my home state of Pennsylvania, 11.5 percent of the workforce is employed by nonprofits (634,098 in 2003), a total significantly higher than the national average of 6.9 percent (Johns Hopkins Nonprofit Employment Data Project, Pennsylvania Nonprofit Employment, 2005). Therefore, I would also like to dedicate this book to every individual who devotes his or her life to assisting others by choosing to work for a nonprofit organization.

Acknowledgments

Specials thanks to my family. My wife, Diane, assisted in many aspects of writing this book and proofread every word. My sons, Jay and Marc, lent their computer expertise. Thanks also to my agent, Sara Camilli, who provided invaluable advice. I also would like to thank all the organizations that, over the years, have invited me to lead workshops and provide assistance.

Contents

Preface

Nearly everything I learned about how to manage an effective nonprofit organization, I learned from serving as a staff member, board member, trainer, and consultant for nonprofit organizations for nearly 40 years. While experience is still the best teacher, there are now myriad books, articles, Websites, workshops, university courses, and even degree programs in nonprofit management.

While in law school, I coauthored a law review article on the legal aspects of the newly formed consumer movement, led by a young, relatively unknown activist, Ralph Nader. Upon graduation in 1966, I applied to the Philadelphia anti-poverty program, that was starting a consumer program and needed a grant writer. While I had no grant writing or anti-poverty program experience, I don't think many others did either because I got the job.

Over the next several years as a staff member, I noticed a dearth of excellent trainers and consultants with expertise in nonprofit management. When I attended workshops, for example, they were invariably led by either businesspersons or university professors with no expertise in nonprofit management. In addition, there seemed to be few individuals who could provide practical consulting assistance to nonprofits in areas such as board development or strategic planning.

So, in 1979, I decided to hang out my shingle and form Sand Associates, a firm specializing in providing training and technical assistance for nonprofit agencies. As I began to work with individuals with expertise in nonprofit fields, I added them to my roster of associates and we now number more than 100.

As I developed a core curriculum of workshops, I gathered numerous handouts for each workshop. My teaching style was to present a series of practical tips for managers in each topic area. Often, workshop attendees, nonprofit clients, and my associates suggested additional practical recommendations from their own experiences. After several years of leading workshops, I developed a core of "groupies," individuals who attended every workshop I led no matter what the topic. One of these individuals suggested that I gather all my tips into a book and give out book chapters as course handouts. You now have the results of my work.

Managers of effective nonprofit organizations are busy people. When they actually list their duties, they often find they have several dozen (including every topic listed in this book, plus numerous others). Some of these duties include serving as spokesperson for the organization, liaison with numerous community organizations, maintaining active membership in local, state, and national organizations, and performing general troubleshooting for the agency. Just being the general communicator and problem-solver with board, staff, and community members is extremely time-consuming.

When nonprofit agency managers have a problem, want to make a change in their agency, or need advice, they need a source of information that gives them practical tips they can refer to and implement in a timely manner. *How to Manage an Effective Nonprofit Organization* is a unique book that will meet this need.

This book contains several hundred practical tips for taking initiatives and solving problems that I developed during my 40 years of working with nonprofits. The appendix includes 17 questions I was asked at workshops, and the answers I provided.

Keep this book by your side and refer to individual chapters when seeking practical advice in areas such as fundraising, board development, grant writing, or strategic planning.

If you want more information about Sand Associates, log on to *www.sandassociates.com*. Of course, I would be delighted to provide training and technical assistance to your agency, or add your suggestions when I lead workshops. Contact me by e-mail at MSand9999@aol.com.

Michael A. Sand

August, 2005

Helpful Tips to Keep in Mind While Reading

As you read this handbook, give special consideration to the following additional tips that can be very helpful in learning how to manage an effective nonprofit organization.

In general, do not say anything, do anything, or write anything down that you would be unhappy (or devastated) seeing in tomorrow's newspaper. This should be a guiding principle for running your organization. (Look how much better off Richard Nixon and Bill Clinton would have been if they had followed my advice.)

♦ Chapter 1—Effective Boards:

"Robert is dead!"

Henry Martyn Robert wrote the first edition of *Robert's Rules of Order* in 1876. My experience is that in most nonprofit organizations, strict application of these rules is used to prolong meetings and make them more complicated, certainly not Mr. Robert's intention.

Each group should adopt its own rules. If certain provisions of *Robert's Rules* make sense, adopt them. If other provisions are too complicated, adopt your own.

(See my suggestion of "Sand's Rules of Order" on pages 49-51.) Try to speak in English, rather than in "Robert's." It is much simpler to suggest to the board chair who is leading the meeting that "I think it's time to vote," rather than "I call the question." All too often in meetings, you do not know whether you are voting on a substantive motion or voting whether to vote.

And when the meeting is over, the chair should simply state that the meeting is adjourned. Asking for a motion to adjourn and then a second and then taking a vote as to who voted for the motion to adjourn the meeting and who voted against, and then putting that vote in the minutes, wastes time and paper.

◆   Chapter 2—Successful Fundraising:

"Plan, plan, and plan some more."

It is essential to spend time in effective planning. Too many organizations wait until the last minute to hold a fundraising event. Then a small group of people frantically starts to sell tickets with little or no planning, or sends out a solicitation letter without giving careful consideration as to whether this is the best fundraising mechanism. Begin the fundraising program well in advance by assigning fundraising tasks to all board and staff members, recruiting community volunteers to help with the fundraising, and developing an annual fundraising calendar with a detailed budget. Only when these and other planning steps are well underway should you begin to actually sell the tickets, call or visit prospective donors, or undertake similar tasks.

◆   Chapter 3—Writing and Funding Grants:

"Write the generic grant."

Nearly every Request for Proposal (RFP) you will ever receive from a potential grant source asks you to outline the problem you are trying to solve or the need of the people in the community for the service. Every RFP asks you to estimate the results of the program you will be operating (or the program objectives). Every funding source asks specifically what activities you will be undertaking with the funds and what the cost will be.

So, begin the grant writing process by writing the "generic grant," which includes all of these sections. For example, you should conduct a Needs Assessment to find out what services the residents of your community need. Then when you obtain an RFP from a possible funding source, you can answer the specific question about the "need" quickly, because you have already completed the research and written a preliminary draft.

- ◆   Chapter 4—Managing Grants:

"Don't wing it."

You are excited that a funding source has agreed to fund your program. But don't begin to implement the program just yet. Find out as much as you can from a representative of the foundation, government agency, or business about its rules on managing the grant. Ask your funding source contact to send you any information on topics such as how you receive funds, how much and when, fiscal and programmatic reporting procedures, and record-keeping requirements. It is better to find out the correct procedures before the program begins than to be criticized later by the funding source for not following its rules correctly, even if you were never informed of them.

- ◆   Chapter 5—Strategic Plans:

"Follow the Plan."

Many nonprofits have started the planning process. They realize the importance of planning for the future.

However, all too often the plan is approved by the board and then it just sits on the shelf. Once the Planning Committee has submitted the plan to the board, don't dissolve the committee. Give the committee the task of implementing the plan. Make certain the plan has measurable objectives. Every three months, review the plan to see if the objectives have been met. When applying for grants, make certain the objectives of the grants are consistent with the strategic plan.

◆   Chapter 6—Being an Effective Supervisor:

"Make sure supervisors supervise."

A supervisor should be orienting workers, delegating tasks, reporting for the unit, calling staff meetings, and performing tasks that will assist the line workers to perform their duties effectively. In many nonprofits, individuals with the title of supervisor don't actually supervise. They just do the work of the agency along with the other workers. Perhaps they received the title of "supervisor" because they perform the work of the agency more effectively than the other employees in the unit. But what they should do is to supervise other employees in the unit and give them guidance.

◆   Chapter 7—Personnel Management Skills:

"Hire great employees."

It pays to spend a great deal of time filling vacancies with excellent employees. This may mean interviewing more applicants than you intended, spending time planning an interviewing process, conducting interviews that are in-depth enough to get as accurate a picture as possible about each applicant's attitude and skills, and preparing an excellent orientation program for each new employee. Time spent firing employees or encouraging major changes in their work habits or attitudes can be extremely painful, often wasteful, and always time-consuming. So, spend as much quality time as you need to help assure your new employees are excellent so you can minimize the time spent changing or firing them.

◆   Chapter 8—Volunteer Programs:

"Do it."

An effective volunteer program can be a godsend for a nonprofit agency. For example, raising $100,000 in grants or through fundraisers can be next to impossible for many agencies. Spending time developing a core of volunteers who provide $100,000 in volunteer service to the agency might be doable. And usually, excellent volunteers both help the agency for a long time and recruit other excellent volunteers, so the services are provided year after year. Of course, while developing and sustaining a corps of volunteers is time-consuming, the benefits are usually worth every minute of your investment.

◆   Chapter 9—Community Coalitions:

"There is power in numbers."

Here is the scenario: Your agency wishes to convince its senator to oppose a bill in the legislature. Which is more effective? Writing a letter from one group representing less than 100 individuals, or writing a letter from a coalition of several groups representing tens of thousands of people. Often having several organizations form a coalition is difficult. But when the name of the game is power, a coalition is the way to go.

Effective Boards of Directors

An excellent nonprofit organization has a well-functioning board of directors. The board has the responsibility of setting policies for the organization and hiring staff to implement these policies. For a board to function effectively, it should meet several criteria:

- Its bylaws are current, are followed, and meet the needs of that organization.

- Procedures are in place for getting excellent board members.

- Steps are taken to keep excellent board members, and to remove board members who are not meeting their responsibilities.

- Board members know their responsibilities and carry them out effectively.

- The board functions through a well-planned committee structure.

- Board meetings are conducted in an efficient manner.

A. Bylaws

Several items should be clearly spelled out in the bylaws:

1. Number of board members

There is no optimum number of board members. The *size* of the board should depend on the specific needs of the organization. If the board's role is limited, a small board might be more appropriate. However, if extensive board time is required for fund-raising, or if the board has a large number of functioning committees, then a much larger board is in order.

The *number* of board members is set in the bylaws. One effective technique is to set a minimum and maximum number of board members and to allow the board to determine its size within these parameters. Then, the board can start small and add members as the need arises.

Another technique is to allow the board chair to appoint a number of individuals to the board with board approval. In this way, if additional board members are needed to meet specific needs, these members can be added quickly.

2. Term lengths and limits

The *term* of board members must be included in the bylaws. Board members should have fixed terms of office. One common practice is for all board members to have three-year terms, with one-third of the members being elected each year.

Having set terms is a good way to assure board continuity. It also provides an effective procedure for removing unproductive board members. At the end of their term, board members who are not productive are simply not renominated.

Some organizations limit the number of terms of board members and officers. If an organization has difficulty finding excellent board members and officers, the number of terms should not be limited. A board member or officer who is functioning effectively should be able to continue to serve. Of course, a board member or officer who is not meeting his or her responsibilities should not be reelected at the end of the term.

However, if an organization has a number of excellent candidates willing to assume board and officer positions, limiting terms might be considered. If the bylaws include term limits, however, it is always a good idea to give the board flexibility. For example, even if a board limits terms of board members or officers, the board should be permitted by majority vote to waive the provision in individual instances.

In addition, not every board member must be a voting member. Many boards include past presidents or current committee chairs as non-voting board members. Other boards include board members or officers who cannot run again (because of term limit provisions) as non-voting board members.

3. Election process

The *election process* should also be clearly spelled out in the bylaws. Many organizations have a Nominating Committee that is responsible for recommending new board members to the full board, and for recommending a slate of officers. The Nominating Committee often is chaired by the immediate past president of the organization, since that individual knows who has contributed to the organization in the past.

The Nominating Committee should carefully review the service record of each individual the committee wishes to consider renominating for either board membership, or for an officer position. Has the potential nominee attended the large majority of board meetings? Has the nominee served as an effective committee member? Have they actively participated in fundraising? Fulfilled their duties as officers? If so, the individual should be renominated. If not, he or she should be thanked for past service, but not be renominated.

Most Nominating Committees recommend only one individual for each board of directors or officer position. This is a decision that should be made by each individual board. Would contested elections help or hurt that particular organization?

Additional candidates for board membership or officer positions can be nominated either in advance or from the floor at the election. In some organizations, the officers are elected by the full membership. In others, the board of directors elects its own officers. Many organizations elect their officers to two-year terms, although one-year terms are quite common.

Boards should also consider forming a standing Board Development Committee and assign this committee the functions previously performed by the Nominating Committee. See Section B, on page 26, for a discussion of the functions of a Board Development Committee.

4. Officers

The elected officers of many organizations are similar:

- **President or Board Chair.** Leads the meetings of the organization. Appoints committee chairs. Either signs or co-signs checks, or delegates this duty to another individual. Often supervises the executive director.

- **Vice-President or Vice-Chair.** Assumes the duties of the president or chair in his or her absence. Often is given specific responsibilities either in the bylaws or by vote. Automatically becomes the next president in many organizations. Many organizations have several vice-chairs with specific duties. A particular vice-chair may oversee the functioning of several committees, for example.

- **Secretary.** Either takes minutes at the board meeting or approves the minutes if taken by another individual. May be responsible for all correspondence relating to board membership.

- ♦ **Treasurer.** Responsible for the finances of the organization. Usually makes financial reports to the board and signs checks.

5. Amendments to bylaws

It is important that each organization has flexibility in changing its bylaws to reflect the needs of that organization.

A Bylaws Committee should meet periodically to review the bylaws and make recommendations for revisions.

A common method of assuring flexibility is to permit the board of directors to revise the bylaws by majority vote at any meeting, as long as the specific wording of the proposed bylaws change is submitted to each member in writing prior to the meeting.

B. Getting good board members

Many organizations are finding it more difficult than ever to get excellent board members. This is due to factors such as the proliferation of nonprofit boards, the fact that individuals often relocate to other communities, and the increasing number of women in the workforce.

Therefore, a board should establish a Board Development Committee as a standing board committee. This committee would assume all the roles played by the Nominating Committee. It would have as its responsibility not only obtaining quality board members, but also of keeping them.

1. Responsibilities of the Board Development Committee

The Board Development Committee should strive for a diverse board and list the types of characteristics desired, such as:

- **Expertise:** Some board members should have personnel management, fiscal, or legal expertise.

- **Ages:** It is helpful to have senior citizens represented as well as young people.

- **Races and religions:** All major races and religions in the community should be represented on a diverse board.

- **Geography:** Individuals should be selected from all parts of the geographic area served by the agency.

- **Income levels:** Having wealthy individuals on the board will help with fund-raising efforts, but individuals with low and moderate incomes should also be included.

- **Backgrounds:** It would be helpful if some board members have corporate backgrounds, some are government leaders, and some serve on the boards of other nonprofit groups.

- **Users of the service:** Boards should include representatives of the client population being served. On some boards, current clients are included, while in others, former clients are considered for board membership.

The Board Development Committee should search throughout the year for individuals with these characteristics. Board and staff members should be encouraged to recommend individuals for board membership. Individuals who have volunteered to serve the organization by assisting in its programs should be considered for board service.

The Board Development Committee should contact community groups to obtain lists of possible board members. Senior citizen groups, youth groups, chambers of commerce, and ethnic organizations could be among those requested to recommend possible board nominees.

2. Board member responsibilities

Each board member should receive a list of responsibilities. These should include:

- Attending board meetings on a regular basis and participating on at least one board committee.

- Personal contribution to fundraising campaigns.

- Participation in board special event fundraising activities.

Prospective board members should be interviewed in person by a member of the Board Development Committee. If possible, they should be interviewed by an individual who knows them. The prospective board member should be asked questions to ascertain if they support the mission of the organization. They should be given the written list of board responsibilities and asked if they would commit to meeting these responsibilities if elected. Only individuals who have agreed to meet these responsibilities should be considered for board membership.

C. Keeping good board members

One technique for keeping good board members is to require all new board members to participate in an *orientation program* before attending their first board meeting. If several new board members are elected, they should attend the orientation program together. Even if one new board member is elected, however, that board member should participate in an orientation program.

1. Review materials

The first step in the orientation process is to review materials that all board members should receive. These would include the following:

- Board member job description.

- Job descriptions of key staff members.

- Bylaws.

- Annual reports.

- Personnel, fiscal, and other board policies.

- Names, addresses, phone numbers, and biographical sketches of board members and key staff members.

- List of committees and committee duties.

- Minutes of last several board meetings.

- Audits, budgets, and recent financial statements.

- List of common abbreviations and terminology.

- Executive director's work plan.

- Annual and long-range plans, and other planning documents.

- Funding applications.

2. Meet with the board chair and the executive director

The second step is a meeting with the board chair and the executive director. This would include:

- A review of the highlights of the materials presented.

- An update of current issues faced by the board.

- A review of the responsibilities of each board member.

- A discussion of board confidentiality policies.

- An outline of the procedures used by the board for discussions and voting.

- A description of the clients served by the agency and the services provided.

- A tour of the office during working hours.

New board members should suggest the committees on which they would like to serve. They should be informed of expectations for financial contributions to the agency. They should also be given the dates of all special events they will be required to support.

3. Other steps to increase board performance

Other steps to encourage productivity of board members include:

- Give board members specific projects.

- Keep board meetings interesting.

- Thank board members for their work.

- Host social events periodically, in addition to formal board meetings.

4. Remove unproductive board members

Remove unproductive board members quickly, and replace them with productive ones. This process includes:

- Bylaws specifying that if any board member misses a certain number of board meetings without a reason, automatic dismissal will result.

- Only reelecting board members who have met their responsibilities.

- Calling inactive board members and asking if there are any problems. In some cases, the board chair should ask for their resignation if the board members do not agree to meet their responsibilities.

D. Governing board responsibilities

Each governing board of directors has the following duties:

1. Personnel

The board's personnel function is extremely important and has numerous facets:

- ◆ **Hiring the executive director.** Procedures for carrying out this function should be spelled out in writing. They would include a job description and salary level for the position. Specific qualifications should be listed. An outline of the steps to be taken to interview and select the executive director should be included.

- ◆ **Supervising the executive director.** Each board should have an effective plan for supervising the executive director. On some boards, the chair plays this role. The board chair should meet regularly with the executive director to review major activities and consult on problems that may arise. On other boards, the executive or Personnel Committee might play this role, and will meet frequently with the executive director.

- ◆ **Evaluating the executive director's performance.** The steps used to evaluate the performance of the executive director should be spelled out in writing. The first step should be the development of measurable objectives agreed to by the executive director and the board. Then, the board, through its Personnel Committee, could meet with the executive director perhaps once every six months. The objectives would be reviewed to determine whether they have been met, and to develop any corrective actions. New objectives would then be set for the next time period.

- ◆ **Developing job descriptions for all staff members.** Each staff member should have a job description that spells out the specific duties of that position, the job qualifications, and the salary. While the executive director hires all staff members, the board approves the job description for these positions.

- **Approving an evaluation plan for all staff members.** While the executive director conducts the performance evaluations of staff members, the evaluations should be conducted according to a written plan approved by the board. As with the executive director, each staff person should have a job description and a set of objectives. An evaluation of whether the employee is meeting these objectives should be held on a regular basis, no less than once each year.

- **Setting personnel policies.** The Personnel Committee should review the written and detailed personnel policies on a regular basis, no less then once every six months. The Personnel Committee would then recommend changes in the personnel policies to the board. Every staff member should have a copy of the current personnel policies. The policies should be reviewed at staff meetings so that the staff members are aware of the policies and can make recommendations for revisions.

2. Finance

The board's financial responsibilities should be outlined in a detailed financial plan that should include the following components:

- **Development of a budget.** Most boards approve a detailed annual budget. In most cases, the budget is prepared by the staff and reviewed in detail by the Finance Committee before being approved by the board.

- **Receipt and expenditure reports.** The board should receive financial reports on a regular basis. The format of each report and the timetable for submission should be outlined in writing. The report should be simple enough that it can be understood by every board member.

- **Fiscal policies.** It is important that all fiscal policies be in writing. These would include such items as policies for salary increases, obtaining travel reimbursement, and procedures for spending funds (such as for equipment, etc.). When are bids needed and how many? What are the procedures if the staff recommends that the lowest bid not be accepted? What are the specific procedures for the expenditures of petty cash?

- **Check signing procedures.** Each board should have written procedures for the signing of checks, including the documentation needed before checks can be signed. It is recommended that all checks be signed by two different individuals.

- **Financial review.** The procedures for review by outside financial professionals should be outlined in writing.

3. Fundraising

The board's fundraising responsibilities should be outlined in a written fundraising plan that includes the following components:

- All funding applications must be submitted to the board in a timely fashion before being submitted to funding sources.

- Each fundraising special event should be approved by the board. The proposal should include a budget for each event, an outline of the tasks to be performed, and a detailed timetable.

- The responsibilities of the board members for fundraising should be spelled out in writing. This might include a requirement to contribute to an annual financial campaign, a statement that attendance at all special events is required, and a statement that each board member must be an active participant in planning at least one fundraising program each year.

4. Planning

Board members approve plans for the organization. They then monitor the effectiveness of the agency's programs to see if the goals outlined in the plans have been met. An overall planning procedure should be approved by the board. This might include:

- **An outline of the planning process.** One common strategy is for a board to approve a three-year strategic plan. The process for development of that plan should be included.

Often the board will establish a Planning Committee to oversee this process. In many agencies, the executive director is responsible for the drafting of the plan under the direction of the Planning Committee.

◆ **Procedures and a timetable for plan review.** In many cases, the Planning Committee will also have the responsibility for plan review. Many boards review their plans every six months. The plan should include measurable objectives so that the review of the plan can determine whether the objectives have been met.

5. Public relations

Another important board function is that of public relations. In order to carry out this function effectively, the board should have a written public relations plan. Such a plan might include:

◆ Development of a general agency brochure.

◆ Plan for newsletters and other methods of informing the public of activities and programs.

◆ Preparation of an annual report which gives detailed information about the agency's accomplishments.

◆ Steps to be taken to update the agency's Website on a regular basis.

◆ Programs to inform the public of the agency's services and accomplishments. Many nonprofits have periodic open houses or public meetings. An annual event to thank volunteers might include an opportunity to inform the public about the agency.

◆   Procedures for working with the media. A written policy should include procedures for answering press inquiries or for making statements to the media.

6. Other responsibilities

Each board should review all of its responsibilities on a regular basis. This might include functions regarding board development as outlined in Section B. In many boards, board members have advisory functions. A lawyer on the board or an individual with fiscal or personnel management skills might advise the executive director in his or her field of expertise. Some boards give board members responsibilities for networking with particular community groups or specific individuals. A board member with ties to a political leader in the community, for example, might meet with that leader on a regular basis to provide information on the organization's needs and accomplishments.

The agency should also develop procedures to give all board members information about the organization's activities. Many boards use frequent e-mails to board members to keep them up-to-date on current issues and programs. Board members then can publicize the agency's programs in the community, refer potential clients to the agency, and correct misconceptions about the agency.

E. Advisory board responsibilities

Many boards are not governing boards but advisory boards. While governing boards hire and fire the executive director, advisory boards do not have this responsibility. Most advisory boards do not have financial responsibilities.

Advisory boards should meet all the responsibilities of governing boards as outlined in Section D except when they are informed that they are not allowed to perform specific responsibilities.

In order to be clear about their duties, advisory boards should take the following steps:

+ Draft a detailed list of responsibilities.

+ Meet with the governing board to review the list.

+ Obtain a written agreement that includes the specific responsibilities of the advisory board.

+ Meet with representatives of the governing board on a regular basis to provide the advice requested.

+ Review the list of responsibilities on a regular basis, and revise it as required.

F. Boards function through effective committees

Effective boards function through an effective committee structure.

- ◆ **Listing of committees.** Begin by listing the committees that are standing committees and thus meet on a regular basis (for example, finance, personnel, fundraising, etc.). Then include the list of committees that are ad-hoc and only meet when needed (for example, bylaws, etc.).

- ◆ **Committee responsibilities.** Include a detailed list of the duties of each committee, the approximate size, and the frequency of their meetings. Circulate this list to all board members and ask them to volunteer to serve on specific committees.

- ◆ **Selection of committee chairs and members.** In many organizations, the board chair appoints the committee chairs and the committee chair appoints all committee members.

- ◆ **Requirements for committee membership.** Some organizations require that committee chairs be board members, while others do not have this requirement. It may be beneficial to permit individuals not on the board to serve on committees. This may allow a committee to add individuals with particular skills, who are not board members. Adding non-board members to committees may also be a good way to see if particular individuals would be interested in, or qualified for, board membership.

• **Assigning staff to assist committees.** It is always a good idea to assign a staff member to advise each committee. For example, the staff member with financial responsibilities would attend all meetings of the board's Finance Committee. The executive director would make these staff assignments. The staff member should also be responsible for drafting proposals. The staff member assigned to the Planning Committee, for example, would draft sections of the plan and submit them to the committee for review.

• **Committee meeting location.** Committees should be flexible as to where they meet. In order for some committees to be effective, face-to-face meetings should be held. Other committees function well by conference call or e-mail.

• **Committee meeting agenda.** Every committee meeting should have a written agenda. When possible, the agenda should be sent in advance of the meeting to all committee members. Then they would have an opportunity to recommend additional items.

• **Frequency of committee meetings.** Here again, flexibility is needed. No committee meeting should ever be held if there is no reason to meet.

- **Committee responsibilities.** Most committees are advisory only. This means that in order for any action to be taken, the recommendations of the committee must be approved at a board meeting. If any committee can take action without board approval, this should be included in the bylaws. Many nonprofit agencies only permit the Executive Committee to take action without board approval.

- **Committee meeting minutes.** Minutes should be taken of all committee meetings. The minutes should include the wording of all motions to be made at the board meeting to approve the specific recommendations of the committee.

- **Membership and functions of the Executive Committee.** Many organizations have an Executive Committee that includes the officers only, or the officers and selected other board members. In some organizations, the Executive Committee is empowered to take action between board meetings. It is important that the membership responsibilities and the powers of the Executive Committee to be spelled out in the bylaws. If the Executive Committee is given the power to take action between board meetings, board members should be notified of any actions the Executive Committee has taken.

G. Holding high-quality board meetings

One key factor in getting and keeping excellent board members is the quality of the board meetings. If board meetings are productive, board members tend to be productive.

1. Planning for the board meeting

An important technique for assuring productive board meetings is to do as much planning *before the board meeting* as possible. This might include:

♦   Sending a notice of the date, time, and location of the meeting to the members several weeks before the meeting. Even if the board meets the same day of each month at the same place and time, a reminder notice is important.

♦   Enclosing as many written items as possible with the meeting notice. This includes:

* Preliminary agenda.
* Minutes of the previous meeting.
* Information or issue papers on important items.
* Executive director's report.
* Committee reports.
* Treasurer's report.

♦   Notifying the board members that if they cannot attend a board meeting, they must call the board chair in advance. In this way, the board chair can get input on important items from individuals who cannot attend the meeting. Also, the board chair will know if a quorum will be present, and can cancel the meeting if this is not the case.

♦ Informing the board members that if they have any items to add to the agenda, they should notify the board chair at least two days before the meeting. In this way, the board chair can prepare for the meeting effectively and minimize surprises at the meeting.

♦ Recommending that the board chair and the executive director meet several days before the board meeting to prepare the final agenda, determine what information still must be collected, and discuss how issues will be presented to the board.

2. Setting the board meeting agenda

The board meeting should start on time. Once members know every board meeting starts promptly, it is much more likely they will arrive promptly.

Each board meeting should start with the distribution of a written detailed agenda listing, in as much detail as possible, with each separate item to be discussed. The board chair begins the meeting by asking the board members if there are any additional agenda items. The chair has the option of referring new items to committees or postponing items until future meetings.

3. Order of business

The order of business at most meetings is as follows:

- **Approval of the minutes of the previous meeting.** A formal vote is needed to approve the minutes. Minutes should be mailed to all members prior to the meeting and should not be read aloud at the meeting. The board should decide how much detail should be included in the minutes. At a minimum the minutes should include:

  * A list of attendees.
  * The exact wording of all board actions.
  * Listing of all votes taken at the meeting.
  * Copies of reports and all written materials.

  Many boards also request that the minutes include detailed listing of all statements made at the meeting. Keeping a record of the discussions is not a legal requirement. One suggestion is for a board to try the "short form" minutes for several board meetings. If the members are pleased, this practice should be continued. However, if board members would like the long version with the full discussions, the secretary should provide the minutes in that format.

- **Board chair's report.** Before each item, the board chair should state which items are informational and which require board action. The board chair should remind members that only policy-making recommendations require board action. The board should not vote on items that are not policy-making.

- **Executive director's report.** This written report should be mailed to the members before the meeting. The board should determine the type of information it would like the executive director to include in the report and the format the executive director should use. At the board meeting, the executive director should inform the board of events occurring after the mailing of the report, highlight important aspects of the report, and answer questions.

- **Committee reports.** Committee reports should be in writing and be mailed to the members before the meeting. If the committee's recommendations are not unanimous, the report should include different points of views. The committee chair should make specific motions when board action is required. Only policy items require board action; no board action is required when the committee chair is simply providing information. The committee chair should ask the board members if there are any questions about the committee's recommendations before a formal vote is taken.

- **Unfinished business.** The only items that belong here are ones raised at previous board meetings. The board chair should remind the members when the item was originally raised and why it was postponed.

- **New business.** Major items of business should have been discussed as part of the board chair's report, executive director's report, or committee reports. At the beginning of the meeting, members are asked if they have additional agenda items. If so, the board chair may raise these items under new business.

- **Good and welfare.** Many organizations provide an opportunity for members and guests to make short announcements, raise issues to be discussed at future meetings, or comment on items of interest.

- **Adjournment.** No formal action is needed. The chair announces the date, time, and place of the next meeting, reminds the members of committee meetings to be scheduled or other steps to be taken, and adjourns the meeting. It is recommended that refreshments be provided. In this way, opportunities for informal discussion and board fellowship are increased.

4. Basic meeting procedures

- All members who wish to speak are recognized by the board chair and speak only to the board chair.

- If board action is required, the member makes a motion concerning an item on the agenda. If the item is not on the agenda, the board chair might postpone the item to a future meeting.

- The motion is seconded by another member.

- The board chair calls on members who wish to discuss the motion. The chair limits discussion to the motion on the floor, and may limit discussion as required.

- The board chair may ask the maker of the motion to revise the motion as needed.

- Once the board chair feels that discussion should be ended, the motion is restated and the vote is taken.

- If a motion requires staff time to implement, the executive director may be requested to state how the motion will be put into practice.

5. Keeping order at board meetings

The board chair's role is to keep order at board meetings. A number of techniques can be used:

- All members speak only to the board chair. When members talk to each other, the chair should remind them to speak only to him or her.

- The board chair informs members if each item on the agenda is a matter of policy or implementation. If it is a policy matter, the discussion begins with a motion and a second. The executive director is asked for a staff recommendation. Board members then are asked to discuss the motion. If the item does not relate to board policy (for example, when it is informational), no board vote should be taken.

- The board chair immediately calls "out of order" any individual who uses offensive speech of any kind, is not speaking about the motion on the floor, or is not focusing on the discussion initiated by the board chair.

- The board chair encourages long-winded members to "get to the point."

- The board chair encourages reticent board members to speak. Individual members may be asked by the board chair if they would like to speak about a particular issue.

- All votes are by hand. The board chair asks all who are in favor of a motion to raise their hands, followed by those who are opposed. The board secretary then notes for the record if a motion is approved or defeated.

- The executive director may receive assignments from the board at the board meeting. It is improper for individual board members to give assignments to any staff member without prior board authorization.

6. Dealing with difficult board members

It is the responsibility of the board chair to deal with board members who are creating difficulties. In some instances, the chair can minimize problems at the meeting. For example, members can be called on for comments only if they wish to speak to motions on the floor. The chair can limit discussion on particular issues.

In other instances, the board chair may have to contact a particular member privately. The chair should give specific examples of conduct that should be changed and also give specific examples of appropriate conduct.

7. "Consensus" method of board decision-making

Many boards take action by the traditional "majority rules" method. If a board of directors votes 8–7 to take action, that board will take the action approved by the majority. Other boards, however, take action only when a consensus has been achieved. That type of board will continue to discuss a proposed action to see if unanimity, or near unanimity, can be achieved.

In this type of board, if a vote is taken and it is a close vote, the board will not automatically take the action voted on by the majority; a discussion will be held about what steps the board should take if any.

8. Sand's rules of order

Each organization has the power to determine its own rules of order to conduct its business. *Robert's Rules of Order* are entirely too complex for nonprofit organizations. So which rules should be adopted? One recommendation is to have each group adopt its own rules.

Because each organization has its own culture, it should adopt whatever rules lead to the business of that organization being conducted in an effective matter. Once the business is conducted effectively, steps should be taken to shorten every meeting.

Following is the author's attempt to develop some meeting rules that lead both to an efficient discussion of agency business and a short meeting.

Sand's Rules of Order

a. No document longer than one page gets handed out at a meeting. Documents longer than a page are mailed or e-mailed to each member prior to the meeting.

b. Nothing gets read aloud at a board meeting. All items are duplicated and distributed to the board members.

c. If a committee has met, its report is in writing and it is distributed to the board members before the meeting.

d. Reports of the executive director, other staff members and consultants, are in writing and are distributed in advance of the meeting.

e. No important item gets discussed at a board meeting without someone having thought about it beforehand. Some items might have been reviewed by a committee before being discussed at a board meeting. Other items might have been carefully reviewed by the board chair or the executive director. If a board member raises an item at a meeting that has not been reviewed prior to the discussion, the board chair refers that matter to the appropriate committee or individual.

f. As items are raised at the board meeting, the chair states if the item requires the setting of board policy. If policy-making, a board member is asked to make a motion before a discussion is held. If the matter requires implementation only, no motion is made. Once the discussion has ended, the issue is referred to the executive director for appropriate staff action.

g. As procedural items are raised at a board meeting, the board chair decides what steps should be followed. The chair might refer an item to a committee, for example, or set a time limit for debate of a particular item. The only time a vote is taken on a procedural item is if a board member requests such a vote.

h. Rules of order are used to help, not to disrupt. The board chair tries to avoid the use of rules to complicate rather than simplify the board decision-making process.

i. All votes are by a simultaneous show of hands. When the board chair requests a vote on a motion, the request is for all in favor to raise their hand and then for all opposed to raise their hand. The secretary can then record the votes.

j. When there is unanimous consent to a board action, no separate vote is taken. The board chair will state: "Do I hear any objection to the motion? If not, the secretary will note unanimous approval."

Boards that adopt their own rules, rather than relying on those contained in *Robert's Rules of Order*, or rules followed by other agencies, find that their board meetings are more productive and usually much shorter.

Chapter 2

Successful Community Fundraising

In these times of increasing community needs and limited resources, nonprofit organizations must spend significant amounts of time and energy raising funds. Each organization should begin by developing and implementing a comprehensive fundraising planning process. This plan should include several components:

- ◆ Outlining the role of board members in the fundraising process.

- ◆ Setting the role of staff members in the fundraising process.

- Encouraging community volunteers to participate actively in fundraising.

- Developing fundraising programs that appeal to the public's charitable nature.

- Planning fundraising appeals that stress the benefits to the giver.

- Instituting an effective public relations campaign that precedes the fundraising efforts.

- Holding an open house to introduce potential donors to your program.

- Analyzing other community fundraising drives and their successes and failures.

- Dividing fundraising prospects into those to visit, those to call, and those to receive a mail solicitation.

- Asking for community investments from businesses.

- Asking for community investments from individuals.

A. Active board participants

For major fundraising to be successful, every board member must be involved in some way. This requirement should be a prerequisite for board membership. When potential board members are recruited for membership, they should be informed that participation in fundraising is required. As fundraising reports are given at board meetings, the requirement for board participation should be stressed.

Board members should be told exactly what fundraising entails. For example, they should be given the dates of special events as soon as these events are planned so that they can put them on their calendars.

One effective way of implementing the requirement of active participation of every board member in fundraising is to list various alternatives for involvement and ask individual board members to choose which tasks they wish to perform. For example, as the planning begins for fundraising, board members might be given the choice of these tasks:

- Serving on the Planning Committee.

- Developing mailing lists.

- Writing a press release.

- Assisting with the mailing.

- Making arrangements with the event site.

- Soliciting ads for the ad book.

- Selling tickets to individuals.

- Visiting companies to encourage sponsorships.

- Volunteering for various tasks on the day of the event.

While all board members should be required to attend all special events, each board member should only be required to select one task from the above list.

In many instances, board members are not convinced of the necessity to be involved in the fundraising process. A board member who is convinced should explain to the other board members why involvement of each board member is a requirement. On some boards, the board chair outlines why active participation of each board member is required; in others, the chair of the Fundraising Committee would have this responsibility.

A specific discussion at a board meeting of board members' roles in fundraising is often effective. In this way, more enthusiastic board members would have an opportunity to convince others. The arguments include the following:

- Successful fundraising takes a great deal of time, so all board members must be involved. As events are planned, estimates should be made of the hours required for successful fundraising.

- Boards should limit the time staff members spend on fundraising so staff members can spend adequate time performing the mission of the agency. While it is tempting to give additional fundraising responsibilities to paid staff members rather than to volunteers, board members should try diligently not to limit agency services because the staff is spending excessive time on fundraising activities.

- For an equal amount of time spent, board members and other volunteers can raise more money than staff members. The general public contributes more readily to nonprofit organizations when the request is made by a volunteer, rather than a paid employee.

* It is difficult to ask the public to contribute to an organization when board members themselves have not made a commitment. Most successful fundraising campaigns begin with a statement that every board member has made a financial commitment to the agency. Program booklets at special events should list all board members. Board members should be introduced at each agency public event as a visual reminder of their commitment.

* Ultimately, board members are responsible for implementing the mission of the organization, and if that requires raising funds, they should be committed to doing so. This is a powerful argument. The board chair might state, "If we are committed to the mission of the agency, and fundraising is required to achieve this mission, then we have no choice but to participate."

B. Active staff members

For major fundraising to be successful, all staff members should be required to participate in fundraising efforts. This should be a policy approved by the board, and every staff member should be aware of exactly what participation entails.

While participation would be mandatory, employees would be paid for their participation. Fundraising responsibilities would be a clearly defined part of every staff member's job description.

When hiring new employees, supervisors should clearly outline fundraising responsibilities. A secretary or book-keeper, for example, should be informed of specific responsibilities in the fundraising area in addition to other responsibilities. The executive director should know his or her specific fundraising duties.

All staff members should be given dates of agency special events as early as possible and should be informed that attendance is mandatory. The agency should have a clear statement of expectations for contributing to fundraising campaigns. While exact donations should not be specified, each staff member should be required to make a donation of some amount.

Certain duties in the fundraising area should be the exclusive responsibilities of board members and of some staff members. For example, requests for major contributions should be made by board members or other volunteers. Individuals who solicit funds at a fundraising dinner, for example, should always be volunteers.

Staff assignments should include:

- Keeping comprehensive records of all contributors and contributions.

- Making certain that checks and cash are deposited in the bank as soon as possible after they are received.

- Keeping accurate bank records of all deposits.

- Developing detailed budgets for every special event.

- Keeping track of receipts and expenditures for all special events and comparing them to budget estimates.

- Making accurate lists of all volunteers and the specific assignments they undertook.

- Keeping the master copy of all funding documents such as brochures and flyers.

C. Active non-board volunteers

Throughout the year, board and staff members should recruit volunteers to assist in fundraising. Because fundraising is extremely time-consuming, a large corps of volunteers is needed to supplement the board and staff members who will assist.

Efforts should be made throughout the year to recruit volunteers. This should precede the decision of what types of special events to hold. When a board is deciding whether to hold a specific special event, the decision-making should include an idea of the volunteers that are likely to help.

Possible sources of fundraising volunteers include:

1. High schools and middle schools

Many schools either require participation in community activities as part of their curriculum, or are receptive to requests from nonprofit organizations. Representatives of the agency should make a formal presentation to a teacher or principal explaining in detail their request for student assistance. Nonprofits recruiting students should emphasize the educational aspects of their programs. For example, a senior citizen center could invite students to a program on aging that discusses the facts and myths regarding the aging process. Then the center could ask students to volunteer for specific fundraising tasks. The agency should be aware, however, that adult supervisors are needed for youth volunteers. The recruiting of the appropriate adult supervisors should precede the call for youth volunteers.

2. Colleges

In many instances, college fraternities and sororities are excellent places to recruit fundraising volunteers. Colleges often will supply lists of student organizations that are receptive to requests for volunteer help. In addition, students earning degrees in particular subject areas are often pleased to volunteer for nonprofits to gain skills. A computer science major, for example, might be willing to set up a computerized record-keeping system for a fundraising campaign. Often, a teacher in a particular discipline will work with a nonprofit organization on a fundraising project. A video class might prepare a fundraising video; a cooking class might volunteer to prepare and serve a meal as part of a special event.

3. Service clubs

All communities have organizations dedicated to community service. These organizations are receptive to proposals from nonprofit groups. A nonprofit is more successful if the request for volunteers or funding comes from a service club member, however. Therefore, the nonprofit should encourage its board and staff members to join community service organizations. Before a specific proposal is made, the nonprofit should review past projects of that civic group. What has been the past involvement of the service group when receiving other similar requests? What are the types of projects to which the service group is likely to commit?

4. Churches

Traditionally, churches and other religious organizations have been excellent sources of volunteer assistance. It is much easier to encourage volunteering if several board and staff members of the organization are also members of that church. It is usually appropriate to begin by scheduling a meeting with the religious leader. Be as specific as possible as to what types of commitments you are requesting. Do you only need volunteers on the day of an event for example, or do you need volunteers to assist in the planning phases? How many volunteers are you requesting? What will these volunteers be expected to do? What type of training will be provided? Many churches will already have committees established to discuss particular requests with you.

5. Businesses

Often, businesses will encourage their employees to volunteer for community organizations or give their employees release time to assist in worthwhile projects. To encourage involvement, a nonprofit should stress the benefit to the business of its employees volunteering to assist in fundraising. For example, if a department store is being solicited for volunteers to help a particular organization's fund-raising efforts, the organization should stress how much money its members spend in that department store. It is always helpful to let the business know in advance how the involvement of that business will be publicized. Letting members of an organization know in a newsletter of the involvement of a particular business or acknowledging the participation of the business at a special event or in a press release can be extremely helpful in encouraging business participation.

6. Senior citizens organizations

Senior citizen groups provide the dual benefits of individuals with extensive experience in fundraising and the time to spend. When making a proposal to a senior citizen group, however, be aware of the limitations of the seniors. Be certain that all activities are handicapped accessible, for example.

Because many senior groups are in need of funds themselves, one other successful technique involves sharing of profits from a fundraiser. It would help greatly in recruiting volunteers from a particular senior citizen club if the nonprofit agreed to contribute a portion of the proceeds to that club.

7. Agency volunteers

Organizations should review their list of agency volunteers for those interested in fundraising. Many times, an individual who assists the agency in substantive areas, such as reading to children in a library, or helping with major mailings, might also be willing to assist in fundraising. It may be appropriate to ask every volunteer who helps with agency projects to also help with fundraising.

Be as specific as possible as to what you are requesting. If you need volunteers to collect tickets at a special event, for example, give as much information as you can as to hours, exact dates, etc.

8. Clients

In certain instances, clients should be asked to volunteer. Season ticket-holders for arts events often volunteer to participate in fundraising. It certainly will not hurt to ask for specific assistance. Recipients of social services can be asked to help in fundraising efforts. In some instances, the agency should keep records of "graduates" from agency programs and ask these individuals for help. Clients are often pleased to assist in fundraising as a way to show their appreciation for the services provided by that agency. Potential volunteers may assist an organization when they are asked to do so by an individual who has benefited from the services provided by that organization.

9. Individuals with special skills

In addition to groups, individuals who have expertise in specific areas should be solicited. Individuals with cooking skills, for example, will often volunteer to cook at an agency special event, even though they have no other connection with that organization. Individuals may also volunteer to baby-sit, serve as an usher, collect tickets, or set up tables even though they may have no prior contact with the organization requesting their services.

Some general rules apply for requesting volunteers to help with fundraising:

- Try to have the request come from an individual who knows the individual being asked to volunteer, rather than from a stranger.

- If the request is made in person, it increases the likelihood that it will be granted. The second choice would be a phone request. If an

e-mail or U.S. mail request for help is made,
it should be followed up by a phone call.

♦ Be as specific as possible about what you are
  requesting. How many hours are required?
  To perform what task or tasks? At what location? What dates?

♦ Stress that training and supervision in carrying out specific tasks will be provided.

♦ Follow up promptly when any individual volunteers. If an individual lists his or her name
  on a volunteer sign-up sheet, for example,
  contact that individual within a day to make
  future arrangements.

D. Programs that appeal to the public's charitable nature

Think carefully about how the funding request is presented to the donor. Individuals will contribute far more
when a particular funding request appeals to their charitable nature. Techniques that appeal to the donor include:

♦ Asking for funds for programs to help those
  who generally need help in society. Programs
  that aid children or the elderly have universal
  appeal.

♦ Stressing in your funding requests when the
  recipients need services through "no fault of
  their own." It is easier to raise funds for victims of natural disasters than for individuals

who have created their own dilemmas (for example, prisoners).

- Highlighting the specific need of the recipients for the services rather than the need of the agency for funds. A request for funds should state that it will enable 25 children to have a special after-school learning program, for example, rather than it will help the agency to overcome a deficit or increase staff salaries.

E. Fundraising appeals that stress the benefits to the giver

In addition to highlighting the benefits to the agency's clients, information should be given on benefits to the donor. Some benefits might include:

- **Tax benefits.** Individuals asking for funds should always be informed of the specific tax benefits to the giver, whether an individual or a corporation.

- **Lower taxes.** If individuals can be assisted to get jobs and "move from the welfare rolls to the tax rolls," taxes will be lower for all citizens.

- **Lower crime.** If young people are in supervised after-school programs, crime in the neighborhood will often be lower.

- **Less time off at work.** Drug-free individuals will miss fewer work days.

- **More jobs.** If a neighborhood has fewer social problems, industries with more well-paying jobs will move in.

- **Increased sales.** As more individuals increase their incomes through better jobs, they will spend more of their income at local businesses.

- **Increased quality of life.** If a community has more cultural events, it will be a more pleasant place to live.

F. An effective public relations strategy that precedes the fundraising campaign

Individuals are more likely to give to an agency when they are aware of the agency's services *before* they are asked for funds. Agencies should develop and implement public relations efforts before fundraising begins, so prospective donors are knowledgeable of the agency and its programs and needs. For example, if businesspeople and wealthy individuals will be asked to contribute to an organization in the future, several steps might be considered *now* to inform them about the agency:

- Invite them to serve on the board.

- Form a business advisory board to advise on policies that affect businesses and to assist with fundraising.

- Develop a high-quality newsletter and send it to potential donors.

- Visit individual businesses to learn about their products and to discuss agency services.

- Meet with potential donors in an informal setting to discuss their particular interests, such as children's programs, services to the elderly, or particular educational services.

G. Hold an open house to introduce potential donors to your program

One effective technique to raise awareness of the agency's needs is to hold an open house. Some tips for a successful program include:

- Invite business leaders and wealthy individuals to serve on the Planning Committee for the event.

- Compile an extensive list of individuals to invite. Asking a member of the Chamber of Commerce to recommend individuals for a mailing list will be helpful.

- Once an invitation has been sent, follow through with phone calls to encourage attendance.

- At the event, make sure each individual is greeted personally to make them feel welcome.

- ◆ Give each attendee a badge with their name and affiliation in large letters so that everyone can greet them appropriately.

- ◆ Make certain that refreshments are included as part of the program. The Planning Committee can determine what type of food and drink would be appropriate, whether a breakfast, a luncheon, or hors d'oeuvres, for example.

- ◆ A short well-planned program led by the board chair is appropriate. A printed outline of the program should be distributed. The program might last a maximum of 30 minutes, for example, and could include:

  * An outline of the agency's main services.
  * Specific examples of how individuals have benefited by participating in the program.
  * A talk by a recipient of the agency's services which highlights the personal benefits of the program.
  * A short video that features the agency's services.
  * A testimonial by a present donor that outlines the reasons why that individual made a financial commitment to that agency.
  * A tour of the agency.

- Decide whether to include a request for funds. Many open house programs just serve to introduce potential donors to the program. The request for funds is made at a later date.

H. Analyze other community fundraising drives and their successes or failures

Very few fundraising ideas are new. In most cases, individuals who have planned fund-raising drives for other organizations will be pleased to discuss their experiences.

In some instances, a meeting with a representative of a nonprofit that has completed a similar fundraising effort in a neighboring community might be effective.

Meet with individuals in person who have had particular fundraising experiences. Ask specific questions such as:

- How many hours of volunteer time were spent?

- What specific services were provided?

- What were the actual profits after deducting all of the expenses?

- Do they have specific recommendations that would increase revenues or decrease expenditures?

- What problems were encountered?

- Can they provide you with copies of their materials, such as fundraising brochures and letters?

I. Divide fundraising prospects into those to visit, those to call, and those to receive a mail solicitation

Extensive research has indicated that encouraging individuals to make major gifts is more successful in person than by phone or mail. Phone calling is not nearly as productive as visiting, but is more profitable than sending a mailing. An effective "phone-a-thon" can not only raise funds but can be fun as well. In addition, many mail campaigns have been successful in raising funds.

Several factors might be considered in determining how to ask potential donors for funds:

- **Prior giving to your organization.** Accurate records should be kept for several years of all gifts to your program.

- **Giving to other organizations.** Lists of contributors at various giving levels are readily available from groups such as universities, arts organizations, hospitals, united ways, and religious organizations.

- **Number of volunteers and their time commitments.** It takes much longer to visit a prospective donor than to call on the phone, so the number of volunteers prepared to make home or office visits and their time commitment is important.

- **Number of prospective donors.** If the donor list is small, for example, a higher percentage of individual visits might be in order.

It is now time to mount a multi-faceted, comprehensive fundraising campaign. Potential donors who are likely to give large amounts should be visited in person by an agency volunteer. Those who are most likely to give in the medium range should be called. The rest of the potential donors should be approached through a mail request. Agencies should consider Website based fundraising as part of their fundraising strategy.

J. Asking for community investments from businesses

Many organizations find that raising funds from businesses in their community is an excellent way to supplement funds from government agencies and other sources. However, effective business fundraising is different from other types of fundraising. Often, businesses have no funding applications or set procedures. Business fundraising, for the most part, is based on personal contacts and requests for funds rather than written grant applications.

Terminology is all-important. The agency is not asking for "charity." Rather, it is asking businesses to make an "investment in the future of the community." Businesses investing in agencies that increase literacy and decrease drug use, for example, benefit several times over, resulting in a higher-quality workforce, in lower taxes, and in individuals with more funds to buy their products. Those asking for money are "investment counselors." Their task is to stress to the business representative why an investment in the community is a wise one.

A nonprofit agency's fundraising committee should take the following steps in their business fundraising campaign:

1. Identify a limited number of target businesses

Businesses on the list to be visited might have the following characteristics:

- Located in your geographic coverage area.

- Sells products or services that your clients purchase.

- Sells products or services that your agency purchases.

- Has a history of giving to nonprofit organizations.

- Individuals in the business have personal contacts with the individuals making the funding requests.

2. Identify a specific individual at the target business to visit

Ideally, the visit would have the following characteristics:

- A board member or other volunteer makes the visit.

- The board member is personally acquainted with the businessperson before the visit.

- The businessperson knows about the services of the agency before the visit.

3. Research

Before the visit, research the following areas:

◆   Products or services the business offers.

◆   Profitability of the company.

◆   Organizations to which the company has previously donated.

◆   Contacts the company has had with the nonprofit.

◆   Information about the contact person at the company.

The agency representative should make an appointment with an individual at the businesses he or she knows on a first-name basis. Businesspeople are busy, so the visitors should plan for a meeting lasting 15 minutes or less.

4. Plan of action

The agency representative should have a plan of action including:

◆   An outline of the specific benefits of making an investment in the future of the community. Provide the number of individuals to be assisted if a particular funding goal is reached.

◆   Asking the businessperson to describe any previous involvement with the nonprofit (for example, they came to an open house or read the agency's newsletter).

- Asking for a specific investment (the "recommended opportunity level"). This number should be the largest amount the business might contribute.

- The businessperson being informed of the specific benefits to the business at each level of giving. For example, a major gift might result in naming a room in a building after a business, while a business making a small gift might obtain a complimentary ad in the agency's newsletter.

K. Asking for community investments from individuals

While some of the same techniques that are effective with businesses can be used with individuals, there are some important differences. Consider these steps when visiting a potential donor's home:

- Call first and arrange a visit when all adults who live in the home are present.

- Learn details about the family, such as the names and ages of children, accomplishments, prior involvement with the agency, participation in the community, and donations to other organizations.

- Prepare a specific key question to ask that would result in the potential donor's involvement in the conversation.

- Have in mind a "recommended opportunity level" to suggest to the donor.

- While in the home, try to arrange a quiet, informal setting.

- Talk briefly about the activities that will occur if fundraising goals are reached.

- Give the potential donor written information about the agency that is well crafted, attractive, and brief.

- Provide written information about specific giving levels that includes benefits for givers at that level.

- Let family members talk for as long as possible, preferably about the services offered by the agency.

- At an appropriate time, suggest a specific giving level. This number should be the largest amount the donor might be expected to contribute.

- Answer any objections to giving at that level in an extremely positive manner.

- Try to obtain a gift commitment at that time, rather than having to follow up.

- Make certain to thank the family before leaving.

- Send a written thank you letter reminding them of their pledge.

L. General thoughts about fundraising

- Not everyone will give or give generously. Do not get discouraged.

- Do not show anger or disappointment. Remember that you and the potential donor still must co-exist in the same community.

- Don't be hesitant about asking for large sums of money. The worst that can happen is that you will be turned down.

- Continue to stress that *you are a volunteer*. Your motivation for seeking these funds is only to assist the clients and the community.

- Make sure to outline the specific advantages to the recipients of the service if sufficient funds are raised.

- Remind donors of the benefits to them.

- Always thank individuals for their donations and for their involvement in helping others.

Chapter 3

Writing Grants and Getting Them Funded

A. Preparing to write grants

These are hard times for nonprofit organizations. Grants from government agencies and foundations are decreasing. At the same time, the number of agencies seeking funds, and the number of citizens in need of the services, are increasing. The time has come for grant writers to develop new strategies for grant writing.

Traditionally, grant writers seeking funds from government agencies wait until they receive a notice from a funding source notifying them of the availability of funds. This notice is called a Request for Proposal (RFP) and includes instructions for applying for the funds and a due date. Grant writers seeking funds from foundations should go to the library, or to a variety of Websites, for a list of foundations that give funds in their geographic area and for the services they provide. They can then mail applications to those that seem to offer the best opportunities for funding.

Invariably, the "due date" for the grant applications to be submitted does not allow enough time for the preparation of comprehensive and well-written grant applications. A new approach is needed. Instead of waiting for the right RFP to come along or locating a possible foundation to which to apply, grant writers should draft a "generic" comprehensive grant for their entire agency.

This approach is realistic because while the format of each RFP seems different, each requests the same basic information:

- What are the needs of the citizens served by the agency?

- What are the objectives of the program?

- What are the services to be provided?

- How will the program be evaluated?

- How much money is being requested?

The development of the "generic grant" should begin by surveying the needs of the individuals in the community for the services the agency provides. Whether the nonprofit provides social services, arts, recreational opportunities, or other needs, it must research the needs of the citizens for these services. A survey may yield this information. Interviews with existing or potential clients may be helpful. Additionally, a new technique is the establishment of focus groups to obtain this information.

Once the needs are established, the next step is to cost out each potential activity or program. It would be essential to know, for example, which activity costs several hundred dollars and which costs several thousand. The board of the nonprofit organization would then discuss the needs and costs and set priorities.

Then the nonprofit would begin to make decisions about where to apply for funds. In some instances, the agency would apply for grants to operate particular programs. The agency then would supplement grant funds received with funds obtained from special events or annual fundraising campaigns.

When the "generic grant" is written and an RFP is received from a government agency, the nonprofit can meet deadlines more easily because much of the text and the budget have already been written. If money becomes available for a day-care center, for example, the agency will already have surveyed the need for a center and will know the costs of operating such a center.

If a nonprofit has determined a need for six different programs, for example, it can then search the foundation directories and apply to one foundation for one type of program, and another foundation to meet a different need. Also, there is no prohibition against applying to several foundations or government agencies for the same funds, so that may be an option as well.

When a possible funding source has been identified that funds a particular type of program, the nonprofit that has already researched the need for that type of program and explored the cost will be far ahead of all the other agencies applying for the same funds.

B. To write a grant or not to write a grant

Because time is always limited, the initial decision must be made about whether to write a grant. Here are some considerations:

Do apply for grants:

- To operate programs to which your board is fully committed.

- To provide services where a quantifiable need has been demonstrated.

- To continue programs that have demonstrated their success.

- To operate programs in which there is an opportunity for multi-year funding.

- To create partnerships when the opportunity exists. Many funding sources emphasize the need for cooperative programs.

Do *not* apply for grants:

- To fund programs, unless you are certain they can be implemented effectively.

- To "balance the budget" in a particular fiscal year.

- To hire permanent staff, unless other sources of funds are available to continue the positions once a particular grant has been completed.

- ◆ Unless the present staff is totally committed to implement the program if it is funded.

C. Grant writing steps

Grant writers should take the following steps before soliciting Requests for Proposals from government agencies, visiting businesses to ask for funds, or looking in foundation directories for grant opportunities:

1. Needs assessment

Conduct a comprehensive needs assessment of the citizens in the coverage area. Surveys, interviews, town meetings, and focus groups are some of the tools used to find what services citizens need.

2. Strategic plan

Develop a plan for meeting the needs of the citizens that includes realistic objectives. The plan must be time-based. List the objectives to be met within the first year of receiving funding, the second year, third, etc. The objectives must be measurable. For example, an objective may be "to serve an average of 100 lunches a day to senior citizens," "to build 50 units of low-income housing," or "to install three new stop lights on Main Street."

3. Activities

Write down the activities to be provided with as much specificity as possible. Include items such as activity schedules, lesson plans for training programs, procedure manuals, and descriptions of equipment.

4. Job descriptions

Include detailed job descriptions for each staff member who will participate in the program. List the tasks in order of the approximate percentage of time to be spent on each. For example, a task that will take 50 percent of an employee's time would be listed first, followed by an activity that would take 15 percent of that employee's time.

5. Evaluation process

Develop an agency-wide evaluation process. Who is participating in the process (for example, board members, staff members, clients)? What will be the main evaluative tools (client interviews, attendance, tests, etc.)?

6. Budget

Institute a budgeting system to cost out each activity. What will be the costs for staff of each program, equipment costs, rental fees, etc.?

D. The search for grants

When all of the information has been gathered and entered on the grant writer's computer, the search can begin for grants.

- Which federal, state, and local governmental funding sources might have grants available to meet the needs of the citizens served by that agency? The Catalogue of Domestic Assistance at *www.cfda.gov* might be a good place to begin.

- Which foundation profiles match the citizens' needs? A good Website to start with is *www.foundationcenter.org*

- Which businesses in the area served by the agency might be encouraged to contribute?

- Meet with your state senator and representative and ask for information on specific funding sources that might fund your program.

- Meet with either your congressman or congresswoman, or a member of his or her staff, in your local district to ask for information about specific federal funding sources.

- Most funding sources list their programs and the application procedures on their Website. Often, the entire RFP can be downloaded.

- Check with similar agencies in your community or other communities and ask for a list of their funding sources.

The grant writer should then ask each potential funding source for an RFP, or any type of funding request instructions not included on the funding agency's Website. Next, the grant writer would revisit the information on the Internet to see what should be included in which specific grant applications.

For example, if the need exists for an after-school program to provide computer learning skills to students, a grant writer might submit a grant to a government agency to get funds to rent space for a school. A foundation could be requested to fund the purchase of classroom supplies. Local businesses might be asked to donate computers and software to the school and to assign staff members to train the students on the use of the computers.

E. Cooperation is the key word in obtaining grant funding

One major factor in increasing the opportunity for obtaining grants is the demonstration of cooperation once the grant is funded.

This cooperation can take numerous forms:

- Several agencies in a community providing similar services can join together. A number of senior citizen centers, AIDS prevention or treatment programs, or mental health agencies can join together to submit a single application.

- Public/private partnerships can be formed. A cooperative crime-fighting program involving both local police departments and social service agencies can be submitted, for example.

- Intergovernmental cooperation should be stressed. Programs that include involvement of federal, state, and local governments, or in which several municipalities are cooperating, are more likely to be funded.

- Total community efforts should be hig lighted. Submitting a program which involves representatives of the business community and faith-based organizations, as well as social service agencies, increases funding chances.

F. Visiting a representative of the funding source

Most grant writers submit grants without ever speaking to a representative of the funding source. In this highly competitive world, a personal meeting with a government agency staff member, a foundation staff member or trustee, or a business official would be highly beneficial. The benefits of such a meeting might be:

- You would have an opportunity to ask specific questions about the grant application that your competitors simply would not ask.

- As you describe your programs, the funding source representative will gain confidence in the ability of your agency to operate programs effectively.

- You can get tips about specific priorities and interests of the funding source.

- The initiative you have taken to visit the funding agency might be helpful when the decision must be made among several funding applications.

You will get the opportunity to ask several questions that will make a major difference in how you write your application, including:

1. How long should the application be?

Ask the funding representative specific questions about the length of previously funded applications. Why write a 30-page application when a three-page application would have been funded? On the other hand, why write a three-page application and not get funded, when a 10-page proposal would have been accepted?

2. Why is the funding source providing the funds?

When applying for a government grant, for example, review the legislative history that led to a funding allocation. When applying for foundation funds, obtain the donor's funding instructions. When seeking funds from businesses, ask for a listing of the types of programs they fund.

3. How much money will be granted, and how many grants will be made?

This will be extremely helpful information if you can obtain it. In many instances, a government agency has a specific allocation of funds for a particular program. Large foundations and many businesses set specific priority areas and indicate the number of grants or the range of grant amounts in that priority area.

4. Can you obtain copies of grant applications that were funded in the previous year?

Perhaps the best indicator of the types of funding applications that will be successful is a review of actual applications that have been funded. A strong argument can be made that government agencies have an obligation to provide you (as a taxpayer) with copies of grants they previously funded. While you may be required to review the applications at the agency's headquarters or to pay for duplication, you should be permitted to review past grants. In some instances, the government agency will provide a list of past grantees and then you would contact the grantees and request a copy of the application.

Foundations are required by law to provide a list of the previous year's grants and a variety of additional information about the foundation and its grant procedures. The lists of grants are available in foundation directories, which can be obtained at the library. Major foundations often have a Website that will provide extensive information about the foundation.

Contact agencies the foundation or the government agency has funded and request a copy of their application. While lists of past grants are often difficult to obtain from businesses, many annual reports and business newsletters include a list of grant awards.

5. Who makes the funding decision and what are their backgrounds?

When writing a grant application, it is important to know who will review it. If the reviewers have extensive expertise in your field, you will not have to define every term. In many instances, however, a foundation trustee or a business official on the Allocations Committee will not have any knowledge of your particular field. You will then have to carefully explain your services in layman's terms, spell out every abbreviation, and define each technical term.

It also will be helpful to meet with the individual who will make the funding decision. When a foundation has a paid staff, the staff person will make specific recommendations as to who should be funded. If a foundation was established by an individual who is living, it is extremely important to request a meeting with that individual. If the donor is deceased, attempt to meet with the donor's spouse, child, or grandchild. When applying to a government agency, try to meet with a mid-level staff member who makes funding recommendations to a department head.

6. What are the criteria to be used in making the grant selection?

Knowing the selection criteria can be crucial in determining how to write a grant. Many grantor agencies have limited amounts of funds and will give preference to smaller grants. Others will make the selection based on non-cost factors and negotiate the cost of the proposal.

Some agencies use "score sheets" when making grant award determinations. The "needs" section of the grant will receive a range of points and the "budget" section will receive another range. Points are then totaled and the applications with the highest totals receive funds. If the agency uses this type of "objective" system, obtaining a copy of the scoring system can be extremely important in obtaining funding. You will clearly know where to place your emphasis when writing the grant.

7. Should you include letters of support?

It takes time to obtain support letters from satisfied clients, from other agencies working with you, and from political leaders. However, the funding source representative should be asked whether these letters may be helpful in making the funding determination. In addition to support letters, a call from a senator or representative might guarantee funding; in other cases, it might doom funding. Knowing in advance, therefore, which calls would be helpful may be an essential funding key.

G. Sections of a grant application

In many instances, the funding source will supply a Request for Proposal (RFP). These are questions to answer when submitting a grant application. Follow the instructions meticulously. If you wish to deviate in any way from the RFP, get written permission from a representative of the funding source. If you are not given instructions, however, the following format might be used:

- Cover Letter.*

- Table of Contents.*

- Summary.*

- Introduction.*

- Need.

- Objectives.

- Methods.

- Evaluation.

- Budget.

- Appendices.*

For large grants only.

1. Cover letter

Write a short cover letter on agency stationery that:

* Is addressed to the individual at the grantor agency whose name, title, agency name, and address are correct.

* Contains a one-sentence description of the proposal.

* Provides the number of participants, jobs obtained, or other units to be funded by the grant.

* Lists the total amount of funds requested.

* Provides the name, mailing and e-mail address, and telephone number of the individual at the agency to contact to request additional information.

2. Table of contents

Grants are not read by funders like one would read a novel, from the beginning to the end. Funders may want to check specific sections, such as the objectives or the budget. The grant writer should make it as easy as possible to locate specific sections of a grant.

Number each page consecutively. Put all the page numbers in the same place on each page (for example, in the middle of the page at the bottom).

Provide a detailed table of contents. In this way, the grant reader can find every section of the grant. Include a description of what is in each appendix (for example, Appendix 4–Letter of Support from Senator John Jones, pg. 42).

3. Summary

For larger grants, providing a summary may be helpful to the funding agency. Keep the summary short, no
more than one page. One factor other than the length of
the grant in deciding whether to include a summary is
whether the grant is innovative. If you are writing a grant
with new and exciting concepts, a summary may increase
your chances of getting funded. On the other hand, many
grants may not include new concepts. If yours is in this
category, you may decide not to include a summary.

4. Introduction

Include in this section important information that
would not appear anywhere else in the grant application.
The following are items you might include:

- The agency's mission.

- Number of years the agency has been providing
  the type of service included in this program.

- Brief history of the agency.

- Major indicators that the agency is capable of
  operating programs efficiently and effectively.

- If there are eligibility requirements in the proposal, a statement that the agency is eligible to
  receive the funds. A statement of nonprofit status under Section 501 (c) of the Internal Rev-
  enue Code should be provided. Most nonprofits
  are tax exempt under Section 501 (c)(3).

- A listing of letters of support from past clients, representatives of cooperating agencies, and legislative officials. (The actual letters should be included as appendices to the application.)

- Statement of how the agency will obtain funding for the program at the end of the grant period. This is an important section. If you are applying for equipment, for example, note that follow-up funding will not be needed. If you are applying for staff positions, indicate how follow-up funding might be obtained. Perhaps this is a pilot program that does not charge fees and, if successful, you would charge a fee for the services.

5. Need

For a grant to be funded, the agency must demonstrate the need of the individuals in the community for the service to be provided. What is the extent of the need and how is it documented?

- The need described should be the need of the individuals in the community for the services, *not* the need of the agency. Estimate the number of individuals who need counseling services rather than stating, "we need a counselor because our agency doesn't have one" or "the funds for the counselor we had were cut back by the government."

- The need should be for your coverage area. While national or statewide figures might be given, if the agency serves a particular county, the estimate of need for that county should be provided.

- The need should be for the particular service to be offered. If the agency provides services for victims of domestic violence, for example, the estimated number of victims of domestic violence should be listed, rather than unemployment figures or other available statistics.

- The need should be quantified. How many individuals are estimated to be eligible for the particular service provided in the coverage area?

Common sources of data are:

- **Census data.** Make sure to use current census data.

- **County planning commissions.** Call your county commissioner's office to find the phone number for the planning commission.

- **State agencies.** The Departments of Education, Health, Labor and Industry, and Welfare are all excellent sources of data. The Board of Assistance (Welfare) and the Bureau of Employment Security (Labor and Industry) may have offices in each county.

- **Local governments.** Local police departments are excellent sources of crime data; local school districts can provide educational information.

- **Self-generated data.** In many cases, an agency can provide the needed data from sources within the agency. Sources include:

  * Waiting lists.
  * Letters from potential clients requesting a service.
  * Information obtained from questionnaires administered to present clients asking them to list other services they might like.
  * Letters complaining that a particular service is not in existence.
  * Testimony at public hearings.
  * Community surveys.

6. Objectives

Objectives are the proposed results of the program. Objectives should have the following characteristics:

- **Time-based.** How many individuals do you estimate will participate in your program in the next three months? Six months? A year?

- **Measurable.** How many individuals do you predict will participate in your program? All objectives are estimates, so select a specific number. State that "we estimate 125 individuals will participate in the program."

- **Realistic.** Do not make up objectives that cannot be achieved if the program were funded. Remember that if the funding source funds your program, the objective you have included often becomes a legal requirement of the program.

- **Countable.** Make sure that the information to measure the objectives can be obtained if you receive funding. Do not list objectives in your proposal if the information to measure them would be difficult or impossible to obtain if the proposal were funded.

7. Methods or activities

Outline the program in this section. Include the six W's of program writing:

- **Who?** Who are the clients? How are they selected? What are the restrictions (for example, age, income, geographic location)? Who are the staff members? When requesting the funding source to pay for new staff members, include a job description and a statement that lists the education, experience, and other job requirements. If applying for funds to continue existing staff, include a resume and a biographical statement for each staff member.

- **What?** What services will be provided? For educational programs, include a course outline. Relevant sections of an operations manual might be included. For other programs, a narrative that outlines the services is appropriate. Still others might provide a "day in the life of a client."

♦ **Where?** Where will the services be provided? Give addresses of all main and field offices. If obtaining new space with the program funds, what type of space is being sought?

♦ **When?** What are the hours and days of the year that services will be provided?

♦ **With whom?** What other agencies provide services? For example, include agencies that refer clients for service. Describe the agencies to which you refer clients. It is important to obtain letters from the other agencies confirming any relationships you describe.

♦ **Why?** Why is your agency providing these services rather than others? Is the agency providing any unique approaches to the provision of services?

8. Evaluation

Inform the funding source that the agency will evaluate the services to be provided.

♦ **Who will participate in the evaluation process?** Outline the participation of board members, staff members, clients, experts in the substantive field, and representatives of the community in the evaluation process.

- **What will be evaluated?** List some of the issues the evaluation team will consider. For example, the evaluators will review whether the need was reduced as a result of providing the services. Were the objectives met? Were the services provided as outlined in the methods section? Will the budget be audited by an outside firm? If not, who will review the receipts and expenditures?

- **What type of evaluation will be provided?** Describe in as much detail as possible how the program will be evaluated. If formal classes are provided, include the pre- and post-test used to evaluate the classes. If a client questionnaire will be used, attach a copy to the application. Describe how the program data will be reviewed in the evaluation process. Include a description of the audit or the process to be used to review the budget items.

9. Budget

Ask the funding source how much financial detail is required. Many funding agencies, for example, may only require the *total* amount you are going to spend. On the other hand, most government agencies require a *line item budget* that includes a detailed estimate of all funds to be spent. Such a budget might be set up to include:

Personnel Costs	Non-Personnel Costs
-Salaries	-Travel
-Fringe benefits	-Space costs
-Consultant	-Equipment
and contract services	-Consumable supplies
	-Other costs

♦ **Matching funds.** Many grants have matching fund requirements. A match of up to 100 percent may be required. Often, the request for proposal just states the match requirement, but does not provide detail as to how the match can be calculated. Contact the funding source and ask if the match must be in cash or may be "in-kind." If an "in-kind" match is permitted, a number of budget items can be included to total the needed match:

* **The cost of all program volunteers.** Use the rate the volunteers would charge if you had to pay them. If an accountant is serving as your board treasurer, for example, include as part of the matching funds the normal fee that accountant charges for his or her services.

* **The marketplace cost of other donated services.** If the agency is not charging rental costs in the program, for example, the in-kind match should include the fair market value of the rental space. If the staff hired by the grant is using the agency's computer, the in-kind match should include what the cost would be to rent that computer.

10. Appendices

Several types of letters of support should be included in each proposal:

- **Letters from potential clients.** It can be help-ful in documenting the need for a particular service to include a letter from an individual requesting the service. A letter from a parent who needs a daycare program in order to ob-tain employment, for example, may be very effective.

- **Letters from cooperating agencies.** Coopera-tion between agencies is helpful in obtaining funding. A letter from an agency head who is prepared to refer clients to your agency if funding is secured can be helpful.

- **Letters from political leaders.** Include letters from federal, state, and local elected officials to show their support for particular programs. Ask the elected official to be as specific as possible in stating how the program would help his or her community.

H. Before you submit the grant

When you have finished writing your grant application, take some final steps before mailing it to the funding source (in plenty of time to meet the application deadline):

- Is it free of industry jargon?

- Are all abbreviations spelled out the first time they are used?

- Have you followed all the instructions in the Request for Proposal (RFP)?

- Are all words spelled correctly? Remember, the computer's spell check only tells whether the word used is an English word, not if it is correctly spelled or grammatically correct.

- Is it interesting to read?

- If you were the grantor agency, would you fund it?

Good luck!

Chapter 4

Managing Grants Once You Get Them

Congratulations! You have been notified that your grant request has been approved. Now you can begin to provide much-needed services. But all too often, the dream of receiving notification that your proposal has been funded turns into a nightmare when you begin to implement that grant. You become tied up in "red tape" that interferes with the provision of services.

Begin the process of grant management by asking the funding source for all written instructions for managing the grant. Read these instructions carefully. You may want to review them with an attorney because they often refer to specific laws or even court decisions. If you are not certain of the meaning of particular sections, ask the funding source for clarification now.

It is best to anticipate problems before even beginning to implement the grant. At this stage, the funding source has selected your agency to provide services and will be totally supportive of your efforts. Both you and the funding source want to see services delivered effectively.

One way to minimize future problems is to request a face-to-face meeting with a representative of the funding source as soon as a grant is funded. By asking key questions and negotiating important items, many difficulties can be avoided.

Following are some issues you might raise to help run a grant efficiently.

A. Receiving program funds

The first key question to ask is: when does the agency receive the program funds and how much will be received? It is important to find out the answer to this question as soon as possible. You would like to begin to purchase equipment and hire staff right away.

It is certainly appropriate to expect that funds from the grant will be received early enough to enable you to write the checks for services provided by that grant.

It is essential to find out whether the funding source will send the funds automatically or whether you have to fill out a form requesting the funds. If the agency must request funds, consider the lead time it takes the funding source to send a check.

How will the funds be received? Some grantors will write a check while others will wire funds directly to your bank.

Strongly urge that your agency should receive funds *before* grant expenditures are made. The agency will then keep records of the grant funds that are expended and the balance in the particular program account.

Be aware that some funding sources have procedures that state that they will not send funds until they have received an invoice indicating that program funds have actually been expended. If a funding source insists on a reimbursement system, ask whose funds should be used to pay the salaries and other expenses until grant funds have been received. Many nonprofit agencies simply do not have the funds to use to pay bills incurred under a new program. If your agency is in this financial situation, explain this to the funding source. If you must borrow funds from the bank to pay salaries, for example, will the funding source reimburse the agency for the interest charges?

B. Program contact

Who is the individual the grantee should call when there are questions? What is the authority of that individual? It is important to have one contact at each funding source who is familiar with you and the program they have funded. You would meet with this individual when the grant is funded so that you can ask the questions that will enable you to manage the grant effectively. As you have problems or questions, you would call this individual. Invite your contact to visit the program when it is in operation.

Once you have developed this relationship, all of your contacts would be with this individual. You would call or e-mail him or her with questions. Your contact would then work with others on his or her staff to get you the information you are requesting.

C. Auditing

Find out all auditing and related fiscal requirements in advance. Before any funds are spent, institute fiscal procedures consistent with the required audit information.

Not all programs require an audit, so ask first if an audit is required. If an audit is required, who selects the auditing firm? Does the funding source provide or select an auditor, or can your agency make that choice? Are there any restrictions on the selection of an auditor? Many funders require that the auditor be different than the accounting firm that keeps the agency books on a regular basis.

Are there specific questions an auditor must ask, or does the auditor decide what questions are asked? What is the time period to be audited? When is the audit due at the funding source? What is to be audited? For example, many agencies require different procedures for recording cash expenditures and tracking in-kind contributions.

Many funding sources will accept a single agency audit no matter when the program year begins and ends. For example, if the fiscal year for one program begins in January, one begins in March, and one begins in July, an auditing firm could conduct a single audit at the end of the calendar year for all three programs. This would greatly reduce the audit cost.

In selecting an auditing firm, a number of items must be kept in mind:

- Does the firm have experience auditing non-profit groups? While numerous firms audit books of profit-making corporations, few have specific experience with nonprofits.

♦ Ask for names and addresses of individuals at nonprofits the auditing firm has served. Contact these individuals and ask if they were pleased with the services of the auditing firm.

♦ Require that the auditing firm meet with you several months before the audit begins. Ask at that early meeting exactly what records must be kept and in what format. The firm may want to assist in setting up the records in a format that will make it easier for you and for them when the audit actually begins.

♦ Require at least a month's notice of the auditor's arrival, the time schedule, and the specific items needed to conduct the audit. There should be no surprises. You want to have adequate time to prepare the appropriate documents.

♦ When the audit firm is ready to draft its report, it should share its findings with the executive director before the report is prepared. The agency's executive director would then have the opportunity to correct any errors or misconceptions on the auditor's part.

♦ When the audit report has been prepared, the executive director should have an opportunity to prepare a written reply. The written reply should be attached to the auditor's report when the report is submitted to the board or to funding sources.

D. Fiscal reporting

The nonprofit should be knowledgeable about fiscal reporting requirements *before* spending any program funds.

- How often must fiscal reports be submitted to the funding source? Funders may require the submission of reports monthly, quarterly, annually, or not at all.

- How much detail is required? Some funding sources only ask for a total of the funds spent, some ask for the total by categories (for example, travel, equipment purchases, etc.), while others require the submission of a detailed line-item report.

- Should the agency develop its own fiscal reporting forms or will the funding source supply the forms and format?

- How are budget changes reported? Many funding sources require the submission of a detailed budget. But in the operation of any grant, the agency might exceed particular estimates of individual expenditures. Can an agency exceed a line item (for instance, for postage or telephone expenses), without obtaining permission to do so from the funding source? If so, by how much?

- If permission must be obtained to exceed a line item or category, what is the format for requesting and obtaining this permission? Will a phone call suffice or must the request be in writing? If the request must be in writing, how much lead time is necessary to permit the funding source adequate time to reply? Even if approval to exceed a line item or category is received by phone, the agency should confirm that approval in writing.

Nonprofit agencies should work with their accountants and funding sources to minimize fiscal problems. Topics to consider might include:

◆ **Uniform chart of accounts.** It is essential for the agency to have a uniform chart of accounts for every grant. For example, if the phone bill is coded Account 403 in one grant, it should be coded Account 403 in all other grants as well.

◆ **Single bank account.** The nonprofit should be able to keep all funds received from all funding sources in the same bank account rather than having to deposit funds from different programs in separate bank accounts. Some agencies set up their procedures in precomputer times when numerous bank accounts might have been necessary for control purposes.

◆ **Single checkbook.** The nonprofit agency should write all checks for all programs from a single checkbook. The requirement for multiple checkbooks also pre-dated the types of fiscal controls that can be instituted with computer record-keeping.

◆ **Single computer-generated reports.** Handwritten ledgers and journals have gone the way of horses and buggies. The agency should use software that generates a single agency-wide computer-generated report that lists receipts and expenditures for every program.

E. Special rules for particular budget expenditures

Most grantor agencies have specific rules that must be followed for particular budget expenditures. It is important to know these rules in advance to avoid audit exceptions. For example, are bids required before a major expenditure can be made? If so, how many? What procedures must a grantee follow when not accepting the lowest bid?

Many funders will not permit the agency to use their funds for capital expenditures. Often, funders have special rules for personnel. For example, if an employee is hired for a particular salary listed in the budget, many funding sources will not permit an increase in that salary without prior permission. Some funding sources impose limitations on hotel or meal costs; others restrict equipment purchases. Agencies awarded short-term grants might not be permitted to purchase any equipment. Often, duplicating machines or automobiles must be rented or leased. Many times, a funding agency will list specific areas for which grants cannot be used (the purchase of alcoholic beverages, etc.).

F. Programmatic reporting requirements

In most instances, when a funding source funds a program, it is are agreeing to provide the funds so that you can offer the specific services you outlined in your proposal. You have submitted a work plan with measurable objectives and detailed program activities. It is important that you know what steps to take when you are not going to accomplish an objective or when you would like to change a program activity.

The first consideration is the notification to the funding source of program accomplishments. How often must a narrative report of program accomplishments be submitted? Requirements differ widely. Some funding sources require written quarterly narrative reports. Others may require a report at the completion of the program. Many funding sources do not require the submission of any reports.

If a written report is required, what is the format? Here again, practices differ widely. Some funding sources permit the agency receiving the funds to determine the format of the narrative report. Others will submit a specific list of questions to be answered or a format to be followed.

What are the procedures to be followed if the agency receiving the funds wishes to make major changes to the objectives or the program activities? Many funding sources have specific procedures to be followed. In many cases, written approval is required from the funding source before any substantial deviation can be made from the original proposal submitted by the agency.

Even if the funding source has no specific rules, it is important to notify the agency providing the funds in writing if you are making major programmatic changes.

In legal terms, the funding source is signing a binding contract to provide funds so that the nonprofit can provide specific services. If the agency is not providing these services, it has violated a contract.

If the nonprofit notifies the funding source of the changes to be made and the reasons for these changes, potential difficulties can be minimized. If the funding source is not notified of changes to the services they have agreed to fund, the funder may demand that the nonprofit return the program funds.

G. General grant requirements

Ask about any other grant requirements. A grantee might require an affirmative action plan, for example. Other funding sources might ask for details about compliance with the Americans With Disabilities Act. Rules dealing with unionization or the payment of prevailing wages are also common. If the agency provides written grant requirements, read them carefully. If you don't understand the requirements, ask the funding source for clarification.

If you are not happy with particular requirements, ask for a meeting with a representative of the funding source before beginning to implement the grant. Outline your position and ask for changes in writing. This is a better strategy than beginning to provide services but not complying with particular grant provisions.

Often, you may need to meet with an attorney to obtain an interpretation of particular grant requirements.

H. Grant continuation

Is the grant refundable? If so, by what date does the application for funds have to be submitted? What information must be included in the application request? Remember, there will be lag time between when a funding application is submitted and when it is reviewed. Make your request for continuation funding as early as you can in order to continue to provide services without interruption.

Some funding sources will grant program extensions if the program funds are not spent by the end of the grant period. Ask at the beginning of the program for the funding agency's policies and procedures for requesting program extensions.

I. Closeout procedures

If the grant is not refunded, what are the closeout procedures? What documents must be submitted to the funding source and by when? If a piece of equipment is purchased under a grant that is not refunded, who has title to the equipment—the grantor or the grantee? If the grantee keeps the title, can it sell the item and keep the proceeds? If funds for a desk were included in a grant that was not refunded, can the funding source send a truck to take away the desk?

J. Fiscal rules

Most funding agencies have special rules for fiscal management including:

- **Interest.** Is the agency required to place grant funds in an interest-bearing account? If the funds are placed in an interest-bearing account, can the agency keep the interest or must it be returned to the funding agency? If the interest must be sent to the funding source, how often must this be done? Are there procedures for requesting that interest be kept by the nonprofit as long as it is used to supplement the program services?

- **Program income.** Can the agency charge for its services? If so, who keeps these funds? Can the agency staff spend their time writing grants to other agencies or raising other funds? If so, who keeps these funds? These are issues that should be resolved before beginning any program. The nonprofit should argue that it should be able to supplement any funds provided by the funding source. If individuals have the ability to pay for program services, the funds received from these individuals should be used to supplement the agency's services. The nonprofit should be encouraged to develop sources of funds to supplement funds provided by the funding agency.

- **Unexpended funds.** What happens to any unexpended funds at the end of the fiscal year?

If funds are not spent at the end of a year, many government agencies require that the funds be returned to the funding source. If the funds must be returned, what is the deadline for the return of the funds?

◆ **Matching funds.** If matching funds are required, are there any requirements for the record-keeping and accounting for the matching funds? Many agencies require an audit of grant cash funds, for example, but not in-kind contributions. What records must be kept by the nonprofit and what records must be submitted to the funding agency?

K. Eligibility records

Many grants have eligibility requirements such as income, age, or location of residence. While the requirements are usually stated in the grant application package, the record-keeping requirements often are not. If a program has income requirements, for example, would a potential client's statement of income be accepted or is verification required? Are there provisions for exceptions in particular instances? What is the specific information you are required to have on file? How many years must eligibility documents be kept? It is important to have all the requirements of the funding source in writing to minimize problems as you implement the grant.

Chapter 5

Devloping a Strategic Plan

"If you don't know where you are going, any plan will do."
—*Peter Drucker*

"You've got to be very careful if you don't know where you are going, because you might not get there."
—*Yogi Berra*

Every organization must plan for the future. It is extremely difficult to decide what to do today if you have no idea where the agency is heading. Before beginning to plan, each agency must make an independent judgment about the plan and the planning process that will work best for them. There are no hard-and-fast rules about how to plan.

Planning is a time-consuming process. Nonprofits must avoid the temptation of taking short-cuts. While a board might hold a retreat to discuss elements of the future, this cannot be a substitute for a carefully thought through planning process.

One effective method is to hold some detailed discussions on the topic "planning how to plan." In some organizations, the executive director and the officers might meet to decide the procedures for developing a planning process that meets the particular needs of the agency. In other organizations, the board might establish a small Planning Committee and assign it this responsibility.

Planning is always a never-ending process. All too often, an agency produces a planning document and then the document sits on the shelf. In an effective organization, however, once the planning document has been developed, a system is set up for comparing the accomplishments of the agency with the specific objectives established in the plan. The planning document must be reviewed and revised on a regular basis so that the specific objectives are meaningful and current.

Specific timetables should be set before planning begins. For example, a Planning Committee might meet once a month for a year to develop a plan. This timetable should be established before the planning begins. All of the participants should be aware of the timetable and commit to meeting it.

It is important to decide in advance the steps that must be taken before the plan is developed, specific processes for the development of the plan, and steps to be taken after the plan has been adopted by the agency's board.

A. Forming the Planning Committee

It is important for each organization to develop a Planning Committee that meets on several occasions to develop the plan. The model under which a staff member simply drafts a plan and then submits the draft to the board for approval has not proven as effective as the model that involves the formation of a Planning Committee. A Planning Committee that meets several times produces a better plan than if the entire board meets just once to discuss the elements of a plan.

The membership of the Planning Committee will vary. Some boards restrict the members of the Planning Committee to board members. In other groups, a wide range of individuals—some board members and some not—sit on the Planning Committee.

Whatever decision the board makes, a plan should include the input of a range of individuals with different roles and backgrounds.

It is important to obtain a commitment from each individual on the Planning Committee to attend all of the meetings. A planning process cannot achieve maximum effectiveness if several of its members miss many of the meetings.

Groups with input should include the following:

- **Board members.** The chair of the Planning Committee should be a board member. This individual can then report to the board at each board meeting on the progress of the Planning Committee. Several other Planning Committee members should be board members as well. This will stress the importance of the planning process as a major board function.

- **Executive director.** The chief executive officer of the organization should be an integral part of the planning process. It is essential for the executive director to attend every meeting of the committee. Often, the executive director will be the individual who will draft the plan.

- **Working staff.** It is important to get input from the staff members who actually perform the day-to-day work of the organization. Think carefully about how the staff should be represented. Perhaps one supervisor should be included and the other representatives of the working staff on the Planning Committee should not be supervisors. If the organization operates several different programs, consider appointing a staff member from each program to the Planning Committee.

- **Clients.** Many groups develop unrealistic plans because they have not developed a mechanism for obtaining input from the users of the service. It is important to include one or more present clients on the Planning Committee. Often an agency will also include an individual who has previously received services and can discuss the specific value of the services received. If many different types of services are provided, individuals who can discuss how each service is delivered should be included in the planning.

- **Other agencies.** Many agencies are part of a continuum of service. Other service providers refer clients to the agency developing the plan, this agency performs a service, and then the client may be referred to another non-profit. It is important to obtain information from other agencies in the service chain. One way of accomplishing this is to include one or more representatives of other community agencies on the Planning Committee.

- **Experts.** In many agencies, it is important to get information from others in the field. This may include academicians, researchers, and others whose job it is to look at the bigger picture. Many agencies include teachers at local universities as part of the planning process.

- **Funding source.** It is essential in the planning process to obtain information from the individuals who provide the necessary resources. While many agencies choose not to have representatives of funding sources sit on the Planning Committee, the funders should have input into the planning process.

- **Volunteers.** If an agency makes effective use of volunteers to provide services on a day-to-day basis, at least one of these volunteers should sit on the Planning Committee.

- **Donors.** Agencies relying on community fundraising should consider including a contributor to the agency on the Planning Committee.

- **Public.** Often, it is helpful to get information from citizens without a specific vested interest in the outcome of the process.

Before making the final appointments to the Planning Committee, it is important to consider the same "diversity" issues as when forming an effective board of directors. A balance must be struck because the Planning Committee should not be so large as to be unwieldy. On the other hand, the committee should be as diverse as the general community it is representing. Several areas to be considered are:

- **Ages.** It is helpful to have senior citizens represented, as well as young people. If the agency serves teenagers, for example, at least one teenager should serve on the Planning Committee.

- **Race and ethnicity.** Representatives of particular groups served by the agency should be included. For example, an organization serving African-Americans should make certain to include African-Americans on the Planning Committee. If the organization serves a Hispanic population, Hispanics should be included on the Planning Committee.

- **Geography.** Representatives on the committee should be selected so that all major geographic areas served by the agency are represented.

- **Income levels.** Having wealthy individuals on the Planning Committee will assist in a discussion of fundraising efforts, but individuals with low and moderate incomes should also be included.

One method of keeping the committee size manageable while including diverse groups is to carefully consider individuals who are representative of several constituencies. The Planning Committee might include a Hispanic teenager for example, as well as a volunteer who is a donor living in a rural section of the coverage area.

B. Deciding who should write the plan

While input for the plan comes from many sources, one individual should be assigned to write the plan. In many agencies, that task is given to the executive director. Larger agencies may have a staff member with specific background and skills in the planning area. In some agencies, a volunteer drafts the plan; in others, an outside consultant is hired to perform this task.

It is essential for the individual assigned to draft the plan to be in attendance at each meeting of the Planning Committee. One early discussion should be the process to be followed. In one model, the drafter submits a draft of each chapter of the plan to the committee. The committee then discusses the draft of that chapter at the next committee meeting. In another model, the committee discusses a particular topic and then the writer drafts a section which incorporates the decisions made by the committee.

C. Elements of the plan

1. Needs assessment

All nonprofits are formed to meet a need in the community they serve. All plans must, therefore, begin with an assessment of that need. What is the need? How many individuals need the services the agency is now providing?

As with grant writing, the need is that of individuals for the specific services provided by the agency in its geographic coverage area.

The need must be quantified. It is not adequate just to state: "There is a major need for the service." It is much more informative to include a statement such as, "We estimate that 750 children in our coverage area meet the income and age guidelines for our Head Start program." If every individual who is eligible for the service came to the office and requested the service, how many individuals would that be?

Needs data can come from many sources including the following:

- **Census data**. Extensive demographic data is available to every agency. Make sure to use the most current census data.

- **Information from advocacy organizations**. In many instances, state and national organizations document the need for the services of local affiliates.

- **Surveys**. Many organizations develop needs information by surveying individuals who live in their coverage area.

- **Information from clients**. Present clients are one "captive" audience. In many situations, information obtained from them is invaluable when predicting future trends. It is also important to obtain information from individuals who previously obtained services from the agency.

- **Data from governmental agencies.** An extensive array of data is available from federal (Departments of HHS, Labor, Justice, HUD), state (Departments of Labor and Industry, Health, Welfare) and local sources (police departments, county planning commission, schools).

2. Evaluation of present services

Effective planning for the future begins with information obtained from the present.

- How many clients does the agency now serve? Agencies must keep accurate records of how many unduplicated clients are seen in a year. How many families are being assisted?

- What are the important demographic characteristics of the clients? Depending on the services the agency offers, information should be compiled on characteristics such as clients' age, sex, race, and income.

- What is the trend data for these characteristics? For example, how many senior citizens are served by the agency this year compared with five years ago? Is the Hispanic population increasing?

- How have clients benefited by receiving services? This is a different question than how many participated. While you want to know how many clients attended a job training class, for example, you also need to know how many individuals obtained and retained meaningful employment as a result of attending the classes. Make certain to quantify this information. The specific benefits to the present clients are essential elements in planning.

3. Information on receipts and expenditures

Planners must have exact budgetary information in a meaningful form. What are the sources of agency funds? What percentage of these funds comes from fees, governmental grants, and special events fundraising?

What are the expenditures? What percentage of the agency's budget is spent on salaries and other personnel costs? What are other major expenditure categories?

Agencies should be able to break receipts and expenditures into specific service categories. If an agency provides three major services, for example, the planners should know what funds are received to support each service, and what funds are spent in each service area.

4. Planning for the future

Now that the Planning Committee has gathered information on the needs of the community for the service, evaluated its present services, and compiled information on receipts and expenditures, the key part of the planning process begins. The agency must begin to plan for the future. This is difficult and has many variables including:

- ◆ **Changes in the community at large.** The future of the agency may be determined by forces beyond its control, such as the economy, plant closings, new housing, changes in birth rates, etc. In our interdependent world, it is important to consider the effects of outside forces.

♦ **Demand for the specific services.** Factors may include the number of other agencies offering the same or similar services. What is your estimate of the number of individuals using your services in future years?

♦ **Funding changes.** Do you anticipate that governmental funding, business funding, or foundation funding will increase, decrease, or stay the same in the future? What is your expectation for future local fundraising efforts?

♦ **Board policy.** Your board may be considering adding new services in the future, or expanding existing ones.

5. Parts of a plan

♦ **Mission.** Each plan should begin with a concise mission statement. What short statement describes the "business of the agency?" Start by reviewing current programs. Every agency program must support the mission.

♦ **Goals.** Each goal is a sub-section of the mission. After stating each goal, consider how it supports the mission.

- **Objectives**. You will be able to recognize an objective because it has the following characteristics:

  * **Time-based**. How many clients do you predict in a week, a month, three months, a year?

  * **Measurable**. Whether the objective measure is numbers of people, tons of food, or hospital beds occupied, the objective must be specific. Remember that all planning objectives are estimates, and it is important to estimate a specific number.

- **Activities**. Many plans include specific activities. Which department is responsible for accomplishing each objective by the end of which time period? Which programs will be undertaken, and which services will be provided?

6. General guidelines for plan development

- **Be as specific as possible**. Because all planning is an educated prediction of the future, guessing specifics is more helpful than guessing generalities. Stating that "We predict that the number of clients will increase by 10 percent next year," is more helpful than saying, "We predict an increase in clients next year."

- **Attempt to cost items out**. If the agency intends to expand in the future, estimate how much additional space will cost (remembering to estimate cost in future dollars rather than present ones).

♦ **Plan for several years in the future.** The length of the plan will depend on the agency. If the agency works in a relatively stable environment, planning 10 years in advance may be realistic. On the other hand, if the community, the clients, and the services change rapidly, planning for more than one year may be problematic. Generally, many agencies seem to be comfortable with a three-year plan.

♦ **Be realistic.** Never include items in the plan without realistic expectations that the plan can be implemented.

7. Getting meaningful planning input

It is important to get meaningful information from a number of different sources:

♦ **Users of the service.** One useful technique is to have volunteers or staff members ask questions to individual clients. Clients can be asked specific questions about services they have received or recommendations for future services. It may also be helpful to ask questions of groups of clients. A meeting of Head Start parents or enrollees in a job training program may be called to get specific planning input.

♦ **Line staff.** Every individual who provides service on a regular basis should be asked for planning input. What recommendations do individual staff members have for the future? This can be accomplished by holding several staff meetings. Another method is to have each worker answer specific planning questions in writing.

+ **Board members.** The board has the responsibility of determining future policies for the agency. Having a mechanism to obtain meaningful input from key board members is essential to the planning process. Holding one or more board meetings exclusively for the purpose of obtaining board input into the planning process is important.

8. Obtaining board approval of the plan

A plan is an extremely important document for a board because it will shape the agency's direction. Steps should be taken to stress its importance:

+ The draft plan should be sent to each board member well in advance of the board meeting at which it will be discussed. If board members have major issues to raise, they should be encouraged to contact the chair of the Planning Committee in advance of the meeting.

+ A separate board meeting should be called to discuss the plan. It simply is too important to discuss the plan as one of numerous items on a full agenda. Often, a full day board retreat is held for the exclusive purpose of discussing the plan.

+ The meeting should begin with the chair of the Planning Committee outlining the major parts of the plan. Even though the board members have read the plan, it is important to hear an oral report. One effective technique is to request the chair of each major committee to report on the parts of the plan that will impact that committee's responsibilities. The board chair should outline parts of the plan that will impact on his or her responsibilities, and the other officers should be invited to do this as well.

♦   The executive director should report on staff input into the draft plan. Do staff members have specific information to report on changes that will be made if the report is adopted?

♦   Board members should be strongly encouraged to have input. It is important for them to "buy in" to the plan so they assume ownership. The board chair may ask specific board members for reactions to parts of the plan. If major changes will be made in a specific neighborhood, for example, board members who are residents of that neighborhood should be asked for their comments.

♦   If major suggestions are made, the plan should be redrafted. Board members should be informed when the next draft will be completed and at which meeting of the board it will be reviewed. The process should not be rushed. If an extra meeting is needed for board members to review the final draft, that meeting should be called.

- ◆ The executive director should outline a staff implementation program. What specific steps will be taken by the staff to implement the plan?

- ◆ The chair of the Planning Committee should outline specific steps that will be taken to provide follow-up once the plan has been adopted.

D. After adopting the plan

It is important for the Planning Committee to continue to meet on a regular basis after the adoption of the plan. In too many agencies, the Planning Committee does not meet after the plan is adopted.

Soon after the plan is adopted by the board, perhaps three months, the Planning Committee should meet. It should begin to compare specific objectives set in the plan with actual objectives that have been accomplished since the plan was adopted. When necessary, the plan should be changed to reflect more realistic objectives.

The Planning Committee should then meet on a regular basis to compare actual accomplishments with those predicted in the plan. Specific meeting dates should be set, no less than quarterly. One other function of the Planning Committee should be to assist other committees in comparing accomplishments with the objectives set in the plan. For example, when the Fundraising Committee meets during the year to review its accomplishments, it compares them to the specific fundraising objectives established in the plan.

The committee should also begin to plan for future years. For example, let us assume that a three-year plan

was established. By the time the first year has been completed, the committee should be prepared to submit a draft
of year four to the board. Then, when year two has been
completed, the committee should submit a draft of year
five to the board. In this way, the nonprofit is constantly
comparing present accomplishments to those outlined in
the plan. In this way, the agency is planning three years in
advance.

Chapter 6

Being an Effective Supervisor

A. General supervisory duties

Many individuals assume supervisory positions without fully appreciating their roles and responsibilities. The role of a supervisor is to "get things done through people." An effective supervisor has the following tasks, among others:

1. Orienting workers

The supervisor should make certain every worker in the unit participates in a comprehensive orientation program. Many organizations conduct formal orientation programs for all new employees on a regular basis. Before employees are assigned to perform specific tasks, they should receive an orientation that includes:

- **An overview of the organization.** Employees need to know the mission of the organization and how their work supports the mission. Who are the other staff members and what roles do they play? Who serves on the board and what is the board's role? This should be done on a face-to-face basis. Each new worker should have the following opportunities:

    * To meet with the board chair.
    * To meet with the executive director and other key staff.
    * To meet everyone in the unit.
    * To spend time in the community meeting existing or potential clients.
    * To visit several units during working hours to obtain first-hand experience of how the agency functions.

- **Information regarding agency policies.** Every new employee should first receive a written copy of each of the agency's policies. Then each policy should be reviewed in detail with that employee by a staff person who is familiar with that area.

    * This process should begin with the *personnel policies*. Enough time must be

set aside for the individual on staff with the most expertise in the personnel area to review the personnel policies in detail with each new employee. The employee should have adequate time to ask questions.

* The personnel policies should clearly outline procedures for disciplining and firing employees. Procedures employees should use to file grievances should be stated clearly. As much detail as possible should be provided on holidays, vacation, sick leave, and other types of leave.

* *Pay and benefits policies* should be reviewed in detail with each employee. A detailed description should be provided of the deductions that will appear on each paycheck. Each benefit should be outlined in enough detail so that each employee is aware of health insurance, workers compensation, and other benefits. This is an area that is complicated and the employee should be given as much information as possible as part of the orientation process.

* The agency's *confidentiality policies* should be given to each employee in writing and reviewed carefully with that employee. The employee should be aware of what information can be discussed with a fellow staff member, what can be discussed with clients, and

what information can be given to the public.

* The agency's *fiscal policies* should be reviewed in detail. What are the specific procedures for being reimbursed for travel and other expenses? Is there a petty cash fund and how can it be accessed?

* The *public information policies* should be reviewed carefully. When a reporter from a local newspaper calls, for example, who should speak to that reporter and what information should be provided?

- **Compliance with the law.** The orientation provides an opportunity to outline various federal and state laws that apply to that agency. In many agencies, an attorney will be assigned this responsibility. Enough time should be set aside so that each employee is aware of important cases and statutes in various areas that will affect how their job is to be performed.

* As an example, an attorney or personnel specialist would review with groups of new employees laws regarding *sexual harassment*. The employees would be given specific information on conduct that is acceptable or not acceptable in that particular agency.

* Laws regarding *affirmative action* and procedures for interrelationships with members of minority groups would be reviewed.

* The Americans with Disabilities Act, and other laws relating to *individuals with disabilities*, would be reviewed with each new employee.
* Current laws regarding requirements for *overtime* and rates of overtime pay would be discussed.

◆ **Information about the general culture of the organization.** The formal orientation provides an excellent opportunity to provide information about numerous informal facets of the agency. An example might be information regarding appropriate dress. Often, agencies do not have a formal dress code. Yet an orientation is an appropriate setting for a discussion of appropriate dress. An agency must be flexible, because different units in the workplace, or even different individuals within a unit, must be permitted to dress differently. A discussion of acceptable standards of conduct could then be held as part of the orientation. This might include a review of appropriate or inappropriate humor within the organization. A discussion of steps being taken to minimize "bullying" in a school setting might lead to a review of appropriate procedures to minimize unacceptable behavior in the workplace.

◆ **Information about specific duties.** Workers must be aware of their specific assignments. To the extent that it is possible, duties should be outlined in writing. A plan should be developed for each worker because some already may be proficient in particular skills, while others may not be. In some instances, the supervisor may show a new worker his or her duties. In other situations, a "lead worker" may be assigned. It takes time to train a new worker; the trainer should have enough time to teach, and the trainee to learn, the necessary skills and duties.

2. Getting assignments

Supervision begins with knowing the work of the unit. Assignments might originally be made by the board of directors or the funding source. The supervisor should meet with the executive director of the agency to get assignments.

The supervisor should be aware of the tasks of each worker in the unit so appropriate decisions can be made about who performs which assignment. Assignments should have clear deadlines.

The employee should also know which decisions must be approved by the supervisor and which can be made without approval. As an employee gains additional experience, the supervisor may increase the decisions that can be made by the employee without getting special permission from the supervisor.

3. Delegating tasks

The supervisor decides who does what. Several factors are involved in delegation:

- **Job descriptions.** Much of the work is assigned according to the job description of each worker in the unit. Care should be taken to assure that job descriptions are current and accurate. Tasks listed on the job description should be specific to each employee, not general tasks each employee holding that title may or may not perform. The task performed most often should be listed first, and the task performed least often should be listed last.

- ◆ **Capability of the staff.** In certain instances, a task may be assigned to the individual or individuals capable of performing it, without regard to whether it is their specific job assignment. If an employee is assigned a new task on a regular basis, however, make certain to change the employee's job description.

- ◆ **Time requirements.** Projects may be assigned to an employee depending on the time requirements of completing a particular task. For example, when a new task must be assigned in a unit, a major factor in making the assignment will be the question of which individual has the time to undertake the duties.

- ◆ **Trust in staff.** Some tasks must be performed perfectly. These tasks should only be assigned to an employee likely to complete them correctly.

- ◆ **Responsibilities of the supervisor.** In some situations, the supervisor is assigned particular tasks and should not delegate them.

4. Coaching

The supervisor should constantly attempt to improve the work quality of each employee. Each supervisor should develop a written "coaching action plan" to help in this task. The plan should begin by listing specific areas in which the employee could improve work performance. The supervisor has a number of options:

- The supervisor might be qualified to show an employee how to perform a task more effectively.

- A fellow worker might be assigned to assist the employee. Make sure that the fellow worker is qualified to teach the new employee how to perform a task. The fact that a worker can perform a task does not necessarily mean this worker is qualified to teach others.

- An outside "expert" might be brought in for a short time to work with the employee.

- The employee might be sent to a formal course or workshop to learn specific skills.

5. Reporting

The supervisor must set up a system for obtaining reports from each worker. Then the supervisor must be able to report on the work of the entire unit to others in the chain of command. In order to obtain appropriate information, the system should include a number of different factors:

- What information should be reported?

- How often should it be reported?

- To whom should the report be made?

- Should the report be given orally, in writing or by e-mail?

6. Scheduling

The supervisor should know the schedule and location of all employees. The supervisor can then give new assignments to even up the workload. It is important for the supervisor to know where each employee is located in case of emergency.

Delegation becomes more efficient if the supervisor is aware of each individual's assignments.

7. Planning

The supervisor should coordinate efforts for future planning after getting input from the workers. Each unit should have a long-range plan with specific and measurable objectives. The supervisor should meet with workers on a regular basis to review and update the objectives.

8. Making decisions

The supervisor should clearly inform each employee which decisions that employee can make without checking with the supervisor, and which decisions only the supervisor can make. Steps should be taken to "empower" employees, to let each employee make as many decisions as possible. The supervisor should meet with each employee regularly to increase the list of decisions each can make. As an employee gains expertise in a particular area, the list of decisions that individual can make should be expanded.

9. Holding staff meetings

The supervisor is responsible for calling staff meetings, setting the agenda, and conducting the meetings.

A tentative agenda should be distributed in advance and should include a list of materials employees should bring to the meeting, and issues to consider. The meeting notice should also list an approximate ending time so employees can plan better. The notice should also indicate procedures an employee can use to recommend items for the agenda.

The only employees who should be invited to any meeting are those who would benefit by attending the meeting. Not every employee should be required to be present for the discussion of every issue.

10. Representing the unit

The supervisor meets with others inside and outside the organization to represent the particular unit. The supervisor should decide on a case-by-case basis whether to go to meetings alone or take others in the unit with him.

11. Solving problems

Many problems, such as those that arise between workers in the unit, become the problem of the supervisor. The supervisor and workers can save time by establishing and following clear procedures for problem-solving. These procedures might include:

- ♦ Setting regular problem-solving meetings with each employee so that non-emergency problems can wait until that meeting to be discussed.

- ♦ Reviewing which problems should be brought to the supervisor's attention, and which should be dealt with in other ways within the organization. For example, certain problems should be solved by the workers themselves and should not be brought to the supervisor's attention.

◆   Outlining the information the supervisor needs in order to solve recurring problems. In many cases, the supervisor will require certain information to be provided in writing before meeting with that employee.

12. Keeping workers informed

The supervisor receives a large amount of information about the work from others inside and outside the organization. The supervisor must decide who in the unit needs to know what, and when, and must inform the workers about information appropriate to them.

A supervisor should let workers know as early as possible about actions that will affect their work. As a general rule, all employees should have input into the decision-making process concerning items that affect their work before that decision has been made.

13. Conducting performance evaluations

A performance evaluation should be a tool for helping *every* worker to improve performance, not only those whose work is unsatisfactory. Excellent performance should be noted as well as inadequate performance. Each employee should have a specific timetable to improve the performance of specific tasks.

B. Dealing with difficult employees

One of the most challenging responsibilities of supervisors is to improve the work habits of difficult employees. Often, poor employees negatively affect the performance of other workers. Improving the performance of bad workers will improve the performance of the entire workforce.

A supervisor can develop an active plan for improving poor performance. It would include the following steps:

- **Document the poor performance.** Write down the details of at least three specific examples of poor performance. If an employee turns in assignments late, for example, give specific due dates. The next three times the employee turns in an assignment late, note the exact time the assignment was turned in. If an employee comes to work late every day, note the exact time the employee began work the next three days. If an employee mistreats clients, write down the exact words the employee used in specific instances during the next three encounters with clients.

- **Think about how performance could be improved.** What are the possible reasons for the bad performance? What possible solutions might there be? For example, an employee might be performing a task poorly because of inadequate training in that task. The problem could be solved by sending that employee to a training program. An employee might come to work late because that individual had to drive their child to a daycare center. Setting up a "flex-time" schedule with that employee might solve the problem of coming in late.

In many instances, an employee has not been shown how to assist clients in an appropriate manner. Having an excellent co-worker demonstrate how to assist a client may solve the problem.

Decide whether you believe the individual is capable of changing behavior. You will take one type of action if you believe the employee simply has a bad attitude but has the capability of performing effectively. You will take quite a different action if you believe the employee is totally incompetent and could never perform the task satisfactorily.

If an employee's performance continues to be unsatisfactory, take the following steps:

- ◆ Ask for a meeting with the employee.

- ◆ Hold the meeting in a private place. If you are meeting in your office, do not take phone calls during the meeting. Many workplaces have a room without a phone where confidential meetings such as this might take place.

- ◆ Tell the employee in advance the approximate length of the meeting so that the meeting can be held without interruption.

- ◆ Begin the meeting by pointing to examples of positive work the employee has performed. It is important to make an employee aware that you may just be discussing one segment of their work and the rest of their work performance is satisfactory.

- Provide specific examples of unsatisfactory performance. Do not use negative terms about the employee or their performance. Just point to the facts. For example, rather than saying, "You are always late" or " If you are late one more time, you will be fired," say, "You arrived at 9:10 a.m. on Monday, 9:40 a.m. on Tuesday, and 9:15 a.m. on Wednesday. Starting time is 9 a.m." If a written report the employee has submitted is unsatisfactory, show the employee the report and point to specific sections that are inaccurate or incomplete.

- Stop talking and listen carefully to the employee's explanation of unsatisfactory performance. Watch their body language. Do not interrupt. If you need additional information, ask short questions and then listen again. For example, if an employee is accused of yelling at a fellow worker and claims they were provoked, ask, "Exactly what were the words Mary used that you say provoked you?" Again, listen carefully to their response without interruption.

- Describe satisfactory performance and how to obtain it realistically. You might say, "When I give you an assignment with a due date and you find that you can't complete the assignment on time, let me know right away. Don't turn in the assignment late without first letting me know to expect it late."

- Ask the employee if he or she needs assistance from you to perform tasks satisfactorily. If they respond affirmatively, try to accommodate their requests. For example, if the employee indicates the need for training to learn how to perform a certain task, attempt to provide the training the employee requests.

- Avoid the urge to comment on the excuses the employee may provide for why the work was not done properly. If the employee indicates they will do the job properly in the future, your comments on why they didn't do the job correctly in the past are superfluous.

- Ask the employee when satisfactory performance will be achieved. Asking "When will you submit that report to me?" is more effective than if *you* select the due date. While you might remind the employee that it is essential the report is submitted by the due date, an employee who sets the date will be more likely to submit the report on time.

- Close the meeting on a positive note. Smile. Shake the employee's hand. Mention some positive tasks the employee has completed. Thank them again for the good work they have performed. Offer again to assist in any way you can to make the work experience valuable for the employee.

Hopefully, their work will improve. However, if the work continues to be unsatisfactory, take the following steps:

- Meet with the employee again and go through the same process as above.

- Make certain the employee understands what appropriate performance is.

- Tell the employee that if satisfactory performance is not achieved, you will move into the formal disciplinary stage.

- Give the employee a copy of the personnel policies and review with them the steps of the formal disciplinary process.

C. Assigning and completing projects

One major part of a supervisor's task is to assign projects and make certain they are completed effectively. Before assigning a project, a supervisor should learn as much information as possible about the project:

1. Origin of project

What was the origin of the project? Did the board of directors originate it? The executive director? Who wants the project undertaken and why?

2. Project objectives

It is extremely helpful to set measurable objectives. The objective might be the number of individuals expected to attend a particular event. It might be the number of booklets to be distributed. Perhaps it is the number of clients placed in jobs.

3. Time frames

By what date should the project be completed? What are the consequences if the project is not completed by the assignment date?

4. Project detail

It will be helpful to the employee to receive as much information as possible about the assignment. If possible, include information in writing so both the supervisor and the worker can minimize communication difficulties.

5. Reporting

Who reports to whom about the project? When is the first report due? What is the timetable for subsequent reports? What is the format of the report? The length?

6. Information needed

Is there information needed before specific activities can begin? Before they can be completed? Who should supply this information? Who should ask for the information?

7. Changes

Who is authorized to make changes to the project without permission? If permission is needed to make changes, who must approve them?

8. Other personnel within the agency

Who should assist in this project? Do they know they are assigned to assist?

9. Other personnel outside of the agency

When assignments are made, involvement of representatives of other agencies should be outlined carefully. Who will have the responsibility of contacting the other agency? What will be the relationship between the employee and the representative of the other agency or agencies?

D. The "team" model of supervision

In the traditional supervisory model, the supervisor assigns the task to workers who report to that supervisor. Each individual completes a task and reports to the supervisor. Yet many supervisors find that this model does not always lead to optimum results. It may be that a number of individuals working together—a team—may be the best way to handle particular tasks. In some instances, a member of the team may be in a different unit and have a different supervisor.

Teams generally outperform individuals acting alone or in larger organizational groupings, especially when performance requires multiple skills, judgment, and experience. In some instances, however, a team may not be appropriate.

1. Should you have a team?

Many factors are involved in deciding whether to have a team:

- **What worked before?** If one individual worked exclusively on a project before, and it worked well, continue that style. There may be no need to give that project to a team.

- **Instructions from your supervisor.** In some instances, your supervisor has reasons to assign a project to a particular individual and does not want a team working on it.

- **Your idea about what works best.** Some organizations do not lend themselves to teams and then there is no reason to create them.

- **Time frame.** In many instances, teams take longer than individuals to complete tasks because of the necessity of getting together. If a project must be performed expeditiously, in some instances a team is not appropriate.

- **Individuals must be willing to work together.** Some employees want to work alone. In other instances, an employee may not want to work with a *particular* individual.

- **The organization or organizations must permit the workers to work together.** In many instances, several individuals on a team may have different supervisors or work for different organizations. Flexibility of each of the work units and organizations involved is essential.

- **All individuals must be willing and able to meet at the same time at the beginning of the project.** Telephone, fax, e-mail, and other communications methods may follow, but a face-to-face meeting with all the participants present is essential to begin the project.

2. Setting the rules of conduct

If a team is to function effectively, several rules of conduct must be agreed to by the members:

- **Attendance.** What will happen if a particular individual cannot attend a meeting? Will it be canceled or proceed without the individual? Who decides?

- **Discussion.** Which topics are appropriate for discussion and which are not? What process is used for making this determination?

- **Agenda.** What is the process for setting the agenda that includes the discussion topics? If a participant would like a topic discussed, how can they assure that item is on the agenda?

- **Decisions.** Who has the authority to decide? Does the group vote? Does majority rule?

- **Confidentiality.** Can all information be divulged to everyone? If not, who can tell what to whom and who cannot tell what to whom? It is important that the confidentiality rules be written and that all the participants understand the rules and abide by them.

- **Specific tasks.** Individuals should know exactly what tasks they have agreed to perform before the next meeting.

- **Deadlines.** No one should leave without a clear understanding of the deadline for each task he or she agrees to undertake.

- **Changes.** In many cases, individuals do not have control over all facets of a project. If they were promised information from another agency, for example, and that information is not forthcoming, whom should they tell and when should they tell?

3. Selecting the leader

One of the first tasks is to select the group leader and define his or her tasks:

- **Pre-arranged selection.** In many instances, the supervisor of a group of people working on a project serves as the team leader because that is his or her job.

- **Assigned team leader.** In some instances, an individual is assigned to be the team leader by a supervisor or a group of supervisors.

- **Group selects leader.** In some teams, the group informally selects its own leader. This may be due to factors such as experience, competence, or leadership qualities. In some situations, the team will select a leader for one part of a project and a different leader for another part.

4. Role of the team leader

While groups vary widely, certain tasks generally fall to the leader:

- Send out an agenda for meetings in advance. The agenda should be as detailed as possible so individuals know what to expect. They should be told which materials to bring to the meeting. If there are major issues to be decided, each participant might be asked to think about specific issues in advance.

- The agenda should include both the starting time and location of any meeting, and an estimated ending time. Individuals should know how much time to clear on their schedule.

- If individuals must prepare items for the agenda, the team leader must give them specific assignments.

- If individuals should think about an item in advance, they should be told.

- The team leader should bring a sufficient quantity of all materials to the meeting.

- At the beginning of the meeting, the team leader should restate the purpose of the meeting and any items of a general nature.

- All ground rules should be restated so they are clear to all participants.

- At the end of the meeting, the leader should clearly restate all assignments and due dates.

- At the end of the meeting, the leader should announce the date, time, and location of the next meeting. Being a supervisor of an effective nonprofit agency is always complicated because of the wide range of responsibilities. Following these recommendations should help to lessen the burden.

Chapter 7

Hiring, Firing, and Other Personnel Management Skills

A. Job descriptions

Excellent personnel management begins with clear and complete job descriptions for all paid staff members and volunteers. Board members as well as paid staff should have written job descriptions outlining their duties and responsibilities.

Job descriptions are recruiting tools because they outline both the job requirements and the duties. They are performance evaluation aids, and should be changed every time job duties change. They are also invaluable when disciplining or firing an employee because they describe the job the employee is "not doing." While there is no standard format for writing a job description, most contain the following sections:

1. Job title

To the greatest extent possible, the job title should reflect the job duties. For example, the job title of the volunteer who assists the secretary in the office should be "Secretarial Assistant" and not simply "Volunteer." The job description of the treasurer of the board should describe the duties of that position.

2. Job summary

Provide one or two sentences that describe the overall function of the position.

3. Responsibilities and duties

Begin with the duty performed most often and end with duties performed irregularly. List all duties the individual performs at least 10 percent of his or her time. Make sure these duties are clearly stated so that a job applicant can understand them.

4. Requirements

List the skills and experience needed for the job. If a particular degree or certificate is required, list it. Rethink these requirements. Many job requirements state that a college degree is required for the job when the agency would gladly hire a candidate who has a number of years of experience, but no college degree. If a degree or certificate is only preferred, state that it is preferred and not that it is required.

5. Name of supervisor

Clearly identify the job holder's supervisor.

B. Advertising the job

Advertise positions widely in order to receive a wide range of resumes. The more resumes you receive, the more likely you will find the candidate you want. Advertising might include:

1. Notifying all present employees

Promoting from within is an excellent tool for promoting staff morale, rewarding excellent work, and increasing your chances of having excellent workers.

2. Placing ads in local newspapers

Agencies advertise their positions in ads in local papers. Often, a community has several weekly newspapers as well as a daily. Advertise the position in neighboring communities as well.

3. Contacting college placement services

Current students and alumni use college placement services to make their availability known.

4. Utilizing newsletters of professional organizations

Often, you can conduct a "nationwide search" to fill a position simply by advertising in the appropriate professional publication.

5. Contacting the state employment office

This is a free service and often pays off in attracting qualified candidates.

C. Hiring process

Carefully review resumes and select the ones that have the requirements outlined in the job description. Perhaps you might select five individuals to interview for each position. While it is not appropriate to call an individual's current employer to obtain information without the employee's permission, a quick call to a former employer can be helpful in the screening process.

Decide on a standardized process for interviewing each candidate. This should include:

1. Interviewers

For some positions, only the supervisor will interview the candidates. In others, a human resource staff person will screen all candidates and permit the supervisor to interview only selected candidates. Another system is for the supervisor to interview all candidates and then to ask his or her supervisor to interview selected individuals. The general rule, however, is that no supervisor should be required to hire an individual whom he or she has not interviewed or recommended.

2. Interview questions

Ask each candidate the same questions. Learn the questions that cannot be asked legally in a job interview. For this, consult your lawyer or personnel specialist. The general rule is that only questions relevant to whether the individual can perform the job tasks can be asked. For example, you should not ask perspective employees their marital status, age, or religion. However, questions about prior experience in performing job tasks listed on the job description are appropriate.

3. Performing specific job skills

To the extent possible, ask each candidate to perform specific job tasks. If a job requires an employee to perform functions on a computer, set up a computer and ask them to perform that function for you. If an individual is being interviewed for a counselor position, set up a role-playing situation where you pretend you are a client and ask them to provide counseling services.

4. Keep notes from each interview

Make notes on each applicant. You may wish to contact references the employee has supplied and also call prior employers. When making an offer, record why this particular applicant was selected and not the others. This document may prove extremely helpful in winning lawsuits filed by those who were not selected.

D. Probationary period

Make certain every position has a specific probationary period and each employee is informed of the duration and consequences of this period. For many positions, it is three months. During this period, the legal requirements for termination are less stringent than after the period has passed. For example, agencies might be able to fire employees without documentation of improper work before the probationary period ends, but not after. Work closely with the employee during the probationary period and terminate their employment if for any reason you are not happy with their work.

E. Performance appraisals

Conduct regular performance appraisals of all employees as standard procedure. Most employees need and want feedback about their performance, especially when it is favorable. This provides supervisors and employees with an opportunity to review and update job descriptions.

All employees can improve some aspect of their work; this provides the opportunity for joint efforts to define areas of improvement. Employees also get an opportunity to discuss how the supervisor and the agency can help them perform their duties more effectively. Performance appraisal meetings should be held on a regular basis, but not less than once every six months. They should be held in a quiet place with no interruptions.

The format should follow this order:

- ◆ **Task review.** The supervisor and employee should review the specific tasks that have been undertaken since the last meeting.

- ◆ **Praise.** The supervisor should point to specific examples of positive work and praise the employee for this work.

- ◆ **Feedback.** The employee should be asked for specific examples of how the supervisor could help the employee perform the duties.

- ◆ **Work improvement.** The supervisor should point to specific examples of tasks that could be improved. If possible, show examples of what improved work would look like.

- ◆ **Timetable for work improvement.** When appropriate, a time should be set for a future meeting to review specific examples of work improvement. If the employee is preparing a written report, for example, set a due date.

- ◆ **Future task list.** The supervisor and employee should agree on specific tasks to be performed before the next performance appraisal meeting.

- ◆ **Follow-up memo.** The supervisor should write the employee a memo after the meeting and list the main points that were made.

F. Formal discipline

No one likes to begin a formal disciplinary process. There will be resistance on the part of the employee. However, if an employee resists attempts to improve work as part of the performance appraisal process, formal discipline may become necessary.

Certain steps should be taken before any formal disciplinary actions are taken:

1. Pre-disciplinary actions

- ◆ Specific disciplinary steps must be outlined in the agency's personnel policies. Infractions should be outlined in detail. The policies should include steps to be taken after each infraction (for example, oral warning, written warning, firing).

- ◆ The employee's job description should be up-to-date and accurate. The discussion can then focus on how the tasks are performed, rather than what the tasks are.

- ◆ A detailed description of the steps taken in the "informal discipline" process should be in writing as part of the record.

- The supervisor should have numerous documented examples of unsatisfactory performance.

2. Supervisor-employee meeting

A meeting between the supervisor and employee should then take place. The following actions should be taken at the meeting:

- The employee should be informed that formal discipline has begun according to the agency's personnel policies.

- The supervisor should not meet with the employee alone. He or she brings another employee (personnel staff, another supervisor) to all subsequent meetings.

- The employee is informed that he or she can bring any other person with them to the meeting as a witness. However, the other individual is not permitted to speak.

- The supervisor should point to numerous specific examples of unsatisfactory performance.

- The supervisor should describe what constitutes satisfactory performance.

- The discussion should focus on when the employee will show evidence of improved performance and what form that performance would take.

- If appropriate, a follow-up meeting should be set to obtain examples of satisfactory performance.

- After the meeting, the supervisor should send the employee a memo specifically noting the points made at the meeting.

G. Termination

Firing an employee is always difficult, not only for the employee, but also for the supervisor and the agency. If an employee has not improved performance after numerous informal and formal disciplinary steps have been taken, firing is often the only viable alternative.

1. Before firing

Before firing an employee, the supervisor should review the documentation. It should then be reviewed with the following individuals before the termination meeting with the employee takes place:

- The supervisor's supervisor.

- The agency's executive director.

- The agency's attorney.

- The chair of the board's personnel committee.

2. Termination meeting

At the termination meeting, the following steps should be taken:

- The supervisor should review the file with the employee one last time. No employee should ever be surprised at being discharged, because the file should contain numerous memos outlining specific steps that have previously been taken to avoid termination.

- The supervisor should specifically outline the termination steps. This includes any severance pay, for example, and the exact amount of time the employee will be given to leave the agency.

- The supervisor should outline any appeal process the employee may have.

- The employee should be given a written termination notice in person.

- Decide in advance how long to give the employee to leave the office. If there is a fear that the employee will be disruptive, give that individual until the end of the day to leave. Make sure they are taking only their personal belongings with them. In other situations, an employee might be given a few days to clear out desks and filing cabinets and for their assignments to be transferred to others.

- Tell the employee you will not inform others of the reasons for the firing.

- Ask the employee not to tell anyone else of the reasons for the firing.

- After the employee leaves the building, immediately tell all employees either in person or by memo that the employee has been asked to leave the agency. Do not give any reasons for your action. If you are pressed, just say that the termination procedures in the personnel policies have been followed and you will continue to protect the confidentiality rights of the terminated employee.

- Avoid the temptation to humiliate an employee who has been terminated. Do not discuss the discharge with anyone who does not need to know and continue to follow confidentiality rules.

- Realize that many employees will not be truthful when describing the reasons for the termination. Yet, the agency must continue to project the confidentiality of personnel information even when the former employee is not being truthful.

Chapter 8

Establishing an Outstanding Volunteer Program

Nonprofit agencies rely on volunteers to supplement paid staff services. Many hire staff members to recruit volunteers, set up special volunteer training sessions, and develop volunteer work assignments.

Unfortunately, in many agencies the volunteer program is given a low priority in the use of resources. Many volunteers are not used to their fullest capacities and are only given routine jobs. Sometimes, volunteers are resented by paid staff members.

Agencies using volunteers are encouraged to institute a different model than one in which a separate recruiting, training, assignment, supervision, and reporting program is established exclusively for volunteers. In this new model, the agency strives to develop an excellent recruiting, training, assignment, supervision, and reporting program for the *entire* agency and to include volunteers in that system.

What are the characteristics of a personnel system of an excellent agency? Such an agency would include the following:

- A system of developing positions with meaningful job duties.

- An excellent recruiting system to find high-quality staff.

- High-quality job training and updating of skills.

- Maximum recognition in terms of pay and other benefits.

- Continuous steps to improve work and to eliminate unproductive work and workers. What modifications would need to be made to assure maximum use of volunteers?

A. Positions with meaningful job duties

In an effective nonprofit agency, an applicant for a position would be given a job description with the following components:

- Job title.

- Job duties.

- Time requirements.

- Job location.

- Qualifications required.

- Training provided.

- Supervision provided.

- Position objectives.

- Reporting requirements.

Each of these elements should be included in information given to a prospective volunteer. Even if an individual is only volunteering a few hours a week, the job description should look exactly like that of a paid worker in a comparable position.

B. An excellent recruiting system

When a vacancy exists in an effective agency, each present board and staff member is given the job description and asked to help in the recruiting process.

Special attention is paid to those who are aware of the work of the agency and have expressed a prior interest in employment. A review is made of the files to obtain the names of individuals who have previously applied. In addition, notices are placed in local newspapers to recruit applicants.

The same system should be used by an agency searching for volunteers. Each board and staff member should be given the job description for each position and asked to "spread the word." Lists of potential volunteers should be kept so when a particular skill is needed, individuals with these skills are contacted.

Lists of present and past agency volunteers, together with their skills and past volunteering records, should be kept. If any agency needs volunteers to bake pies for a special event, for example, a list of individuals who had baked pies for the agency previously should be checked.

Notices of volunteer opportunities should be placed in local newspapers, placement offices in local colleges, and the bulletin board of the agency. In addition, volunteer recruitment should be an ongoing process during the year.

Requests for volunteers (including the job description) should be placed on the agency's Website.

Many agencies hold an open house when looking for volunteers. Often, when individuals see the good work of an agency first-hand and meet enthusiastic board and staff members, they are likely to volunteer.

Staff should take the job descriptions for the available positions to various groups in the community including:

- **Volunteer Centers.** Many communities have organizations that match potential volunteers with agencies seeking volunteers.

- **Retired and Senior Volunteer Programs (RSVP).** Local RSVP programs are an excellent source of volunteers.

- **Businesses.** A growing number of businesses have specific programs to match their employees with programs seeking volunteers.

- **Schools.** Many middle schools and high schools encourage their students to participate in volunteer activities.

- **Churches.** Religious organizations have traditionally encouraged their congregants to volunteer for community service programs.

- **Community Service Organizations.** Every time a staff or board member either speaks at a meeting of a service organization, or attends one of its meetings, a request for volunteers would be appropriate. Some organizations will provide their mailing lists and support your efforts to request volunteer assistance.

C. High-quality job training and updating of skills

Every new worker in an agency should participate in an orientation program to learn about the agency's mission, goals, objectives, procedures, staffing capabilities, budgets, and interrelationships.

Workers are then provided with detailed instructions on how their particular positions are to be performed. A fellow worker or a supervisor is assigned to work with each new employee to answer questions and help improve job performance. Additional training is provided, such as the opportunity to participate in training sessions offered by the professional association to which the agency belongs.

Volunteers should be included in this orientation and training system along with paid workers. To perform effectively, they must be given the same information about the agency that paid staff members receive. They must be shown what their job entails and be helped to improve their performance. They also should be given special opportunities to improve their skills by taking advantage of additional training.

Volunteers should receive information about procedures to follow when not completing an assignment for which they have volunteered. In some cases, volunteers are permitted to miss assignments; in other situations they must obtain replacements if they cannot complete an assignment.

D. Maximum recognition in terms of pay and other benefits

An excellent agency attempts to maximize the benefits of working for that agency. These benefits might include:

- Salary and fringe benefits appropriate to that position.

- The satisfaction of performing duties that help individuals in the community live better lives.

- The opportunity to improve skills by participating in training programs both inside and outside the agency.

- Constant praise, both in the office and in public, for work well done.

- The opportunity for fellowship with other workers, both at work and in the community.

♦ The opportunity to obtain high-quality references that will lead to employment advancement.

Volunteers have chosen to provide their services to an organization with the understanding that they will not receive monetary compensation. An agency wishing for excellent volunteers will provide numerous other benefits.

Examples may include:

1. On-site training

Volunteers should participate in the agency's formal training and orientation programs and receive training from their supervisor and other co-workers.

2. Off-site training

Volunteers should be able to attend conferences and training programs that would enable them to improve their skills.

3. Internal praise

Executives, supervisors, and other paid staff should constantly praise volunteers for effective work.

4. External praise

Volunteers should be recognized at dinners and other public occasions, and stories about their accomplishments should appear in newspaper articles, agency newsletters, and other publicity organs. Information about volunteer opportunities and profiles of individual agency volunteers should always be included on the agency's Website.

5. Fellowship

Special care should be taken to include volunteers in lunch plans, parties, and other agency social gatherings. They should be included in staff meetings and invited to attend board meetings from time to time to meet board members and see how policies are made.

6. References

Volunteers should receive reference letters for the work they have performed and be encouraged to list agency staff members as references when searching for employment opportunities.

E. Improve work and eliminate unproductive work and workers

An excellent agency constantly takes steps to improve work quality by providing volunteers high-quality supervision and training opportunities. Workers are praised for excellent work and are encouraged to improve their skills.

If a volunteer is not performing satisfactorily, the supervisor should meet with that individual privately. The meeting should follow the following format:

- The supervisor should point to several specific examples of unsatisfactory performance.

- The volunteer should be informed that once he or she volunteers, that individual represents the agency to the public and will be held to the same standards as paid workers.

- Examples of satisfactory work should be provided.

- The volunteer should be asked if he or she is willing to perform the work as outlined by the supervisor.

- If the volunteer agrees to the requests of the supervisor, the meeting should end on a positive note.

- If the volunteer does not agree, the supervisor has the option to inform the volunteer that he or she may no longer perform tasks for the agency.

Agencies wishing to derive maximum benefits from volunteers first should review their policies to make certain to maximize the opportunities for paid workers to have fulfilling work experiences. Then, the agency should integrate volunteers into the workforce.

All staff members should be informed that volunteers will be treated the same as paid staff members. The position of volunteer coordinator should be expanded to include the role of serving as an advocate for the integration of volunteers into the workforce.

Chapter 9

Forming Community Coalitions That Work

"We must all hang together, or assuredly we shall all hang separately."
—Benjamin Franklin

While Ben Franklin uttered these words in 1776 in quite a different context, they can be relevant to community organizations today. As the needs of citizens increase much faster than the funds available to meet those needs, the importance of nonprofit organizations

181

joining together also increases. In addition, coalitions of social service organizations, businesses, churches, governmental agencies, and other groups form to meet community needs. Many funding sources are giving priority to coalitions when making funding allocations.

A. Types of coalition projects

What types of projects can community coalitions undertake? Here are a few:

1. Development of a referral network

No single agency provides clients with every service they need. Individuals visit agencies that provide some services and refer clients to other agencies to receive additional services. It is important that representatives of different agencies meet to establish a coordinated services network. They then can discuss common issues and identify gaps in services.

2. Forum for discussing common issues

All agencies in a community are impacted by common events (for example, distress caused by a major plant closing, problems and opportunities created by federal "welfare reform" legislation, or the need to work together to assist multi-problem families). It is important for groups to meet on a regular basis to discuss common issues.

3. Sharing joint resources

Agencies can profit financially by joining with others (for example, joint purchasing, training in common areas of interest, holding a single conference rather than many separate ones). Many agencies are profiting financially from joint fundraising efforts. They find that they can raise more money for each agency jointly than each agency could raise individually.

4. Joint legislative advocacy

In many instances, a single agency does not have the power to promote favorable legislation at the local or state level, or to oppose unfavorable legislation; a joint coalition will have more clout. Legislators are much more likely to respond to requests when they know that numerous agencies and large numbers of constituents are supporting the recommended changes.

5. Networking

Many individuals who join coalitions state that a major benefit is meeting other individuals they might not otherwise meet. Getting the opportunity to become friendly with the superintendent of schools or the CEO of the largest business in town is important to any agency executive. Progress in problem-solving becomes much easier when you know personally other individuals who can assist. Just being able reach others quickly may be important in many situations.

6. Joint funding opportunities

Many federal and state funding sources give priority to coalitions when funding community projects. In addition, sharing information on funding opportunities may be helpful to individual members of the coalition. If a project comes with a $25,000 price tag, having five agencies meet and each pledge $5,000 may solve the funding problem in instances when getting a $25,000 grant or having a single agency contribute that sum is not feasible.

7. Sharing information

It may be helpful to meet to share information about services, training opportunities, or new techniques. In many instances, this will lead to further joint efforts, such as a conference on a particular topic. Information about how individuals solved a common problem may be helpful. Having individuals meet to discuss issues is often more effective than if individuals talk on the phone or exchange views by e-mail.

8. Discussions of community-wide problems

Many problems can only be solved effectively if attacked by numerous community groups with different roles. In numerous communities with a drug abuse problem, a school or business will often try to solve the problem by itself. The drug problem certainly could be more easily dealt with by a community coalition comprised of representatives from law enforcement agencies, religious organizations, businesses, social service agencies, hospitals, and political leaders.

B. Problems

If community coalitions can be successful in so many areas, why don't numerous models exist in every community? Problems in forming and sustaining coalitions can be major:

1. Overload

Many staff members are simply too busy to attend the meetings necessary to achieve community cooperation.

2. Turf

Some agencies are so protective of their service area that they will not meet with others providing similar services.

3. Lack of resources

Some partnerships do not succeed because of lack of funds for items such as postage, duplicating, telephone costs, etc.

4. Lack of leadership

Many coalitions fail because no leaders emerge to frame issues, run meetings effectively, or develop action plans.

5. Lack of interest in others' problems

In many instances, an agency only participates in a coalition if it deals with "their" issues. An agency not interested in economic development, for example, may lose interest when the coalition begins an economic development project.

6. Difficulty in dealing with different philosophies

It is often difficult to cooperate with individuals who do not agree with you. Developing a strategy for helping low-income citizens becomes problematic, for example, when there is genuine disagreement concerning the causes and cures for poverty.

7. Having different attendees at every meeting

It is extremely difficult to sustain a coalition without a core groups of individuals who are present for each meeting.

C. Solutions to coalition-building problems

Because there are problems in forming coalitions, we must be even more diligent when forming them. Some solutions to overcoming common problems include:

1. Meeting with those who want to meet

For numerous reasons, not all "players" wish to come to the same table. Begin with those who are ready to participate, rather than waiting for full participation. If coalition projects are successful, individuals who are reluctant at first may be quite willing to participate at a later date.

2. Starting small

It is difficult to achieve major objectives immediately. Start by achieving small ones, such as writing a joint letter to support a bill in the legislature, or listening to a talk by a coalition leader in another community. Once small victories have been achieved, coalitions are more likely to succeed in dealing with major issues.

3. Selecting projects with wide interest

Individuals will tend to work on projects in which they have a direct interest. It is important to select projects that interest all of the coalition participants.

4. Calling in advance of meetings

Everyone is busy and must set priorities for attending meetings. Call attendees to encourage them to attend rather than only sending a written notice.

5. Beginning with action items; saving "structure" for later

Organizations spend too much time hammering out bylaws and other procedural matters. Action steps should be taken first; bylaws can be developed later.

6. Giving attendees specific assignments

In many instances, an individual given an important assignment will be much more likely to attend subsequent meetings when their "report" is due.

7. Working on "fun" projects

Some projects are long-range and tedious. Other are more enjoyable. Working on a joint picnic will attract more individuals than working on housing code regulations.

8. Setting a date and agenda for the next meeting

Ask the participants to bring their calendars with them. Then before the meeting ends, discuss a specific date, place, and time for the next meeting.

9. Feeding the participants

"If you feed them, they will come" is an excellent adage for community-building. Serving delicious lunches, for example, is known to increase attendance. Even providing coffee, sodas, and snacks throughout the meeting can be helpful.

Conclusion

Is it easy to manage an effective nonprofit organization? The answer to that question is easy. No.

Providing high-quality services to the target population, serving the needs of the community, managing with limited resources, and supervising staff members who are often overworked and underpaid is never easy, no matter what the needs or the resources.

Are there tips to make it less stressful to manage a nonprofit agency? Certainly.

- ♦ **Surround yourself with excellent people.**
  Spending time to hire, train, and retain high-quality staff members is time well spent.

- **A high-quality board with all members who are dedicated to assisting the agency can make the job of managing the agency significantly easier.** An effective manager spends significant amounts of time on board development.

- **Make sure the mission of the agency is clear to all board, staff, volunteers, and community members.** Then, operate programs that are consistent with the mission.

- **Communicate, communicate, communicate.** When a problem arises, whether with a board, staff, or community person, deal with it. Ask questions. Get answers. Solve problems.

- **Keep your eye on the prize.** Continue to strive for excellence. Resist the temptation to do less than excellent work. While often your striving will not be appreciated, you will be a better person and the world will be a better place.

Questions and Answers

Introduction

The style I have used in leading more than a thousand workshops for nonprofit organizations in my career is to welcome questions throughout the workshop.

I tell every group two things before beginning my presentation. "There are no silly questions." If a participant has a question, he or she should ask it. In all probability, many other individuals were going to ask the same question. Also, my answer to most questions is, "It depends." There are very few questions about nonprofit management that can be answered with a yes or no.

By using this technique, participants ask numerous questions. I find that I learn from the questions, and I am certain the "students" do, too. Many of the "tips" included in the text of this book were suggested by the class participants.

I felt it would be helpful to provide some of the questions I have been asked over the years, and the answers I have given (to the best of my recollection).

Question 1: Board development

What role should the executive director play when a motion is made at a board meeting to set board policy?

Reply: Whenever a motion is made at a board meeting to set policy, the board chair should ask the executive director (ED) whether he or she would like to express an opinion on the motion. While it is not necessary for the ED to speak, it is important to ask if the ED would like to speak. If the motion could have an effect on the staff, often the ED will want to outline to the board what that effect might be.

Question 2: Board development

If the ED makes a recommendation on a matter of board policy, how often should the board follow the recommendation of the ED?

Reply: I am often asked this question and once replied "84 percent." If the board always followed the ED's recommendation, the board would not be functioning properly.

While the board should carefully consider the ED's recommendation, the board represents the community, and the position of the board may differ from the ED's position from time to time.

If, however, the board rarely follows the ED's recommendation, that also indicates a problem, either with the board, or with the ED. If the board and the ED are both meeting their responsibilities, the board should be following the ED's recommendations most of the time.

Question 3: Board development

What should the staff do if the executive director makes a recommendation on a matter of board policy, the board doesn't follow it, and the staff is terribly unhappy?

Reply: The staff should carry out board policy except in the rare instance when staff members are asked to do something illegal. In this case, staff members should consult the agency's attorney who will recommend appropriate action. Staff members should be reminded that the board sets policy for the agency, not the staff.

Question 4: Board development

What happens if board members give assignments directly to staff members?

Reply: Board members should not generally give assignments to staff members. If a board member gives an assignment to any staff member, the staff member should ask his or her supervisor what action to take. The board chair should explain to the board member that staff members should only receive assignments from their supervisor. The one major exception to this rule is that the ED receives assignments from the board at board meetings, and from whoever is assigned by the board to serve as the ED's supervisor.

Question 5: Board development

I am the executive director of a nonprofit agency. If a board member is disruptive at several board meetings, what should I do?

Reply: First and foremost, staff members should never criticize the behavior of board members in a public setting. That can lose you your job quickly. It may be appropriate for you to make some private suggestions to your board chair in private, especially if he or she seems receptive to the discussion. Some suggestions might be:

*   See when the board member's term ends.
    Then take steps to encourage the board not
    to reelect that individual.

♦ Suggest that the board chair write down examples of inappropriate behavior.

♦ The board chair might meet with the board member, describe the behavior, and suggest appropriate behavior. For example, the chair might say, "John, you talked for more than a half hour in favor of the motion you made. Perhaps you could just jot down the points you wish to make and then you could make the points more clearly and take up less time."

♦ Suggest to a good friend of the board member that the friend discuss the inappropriate behavior privately with the board member.

♦ Recommend to the board chair that criticizing any board member's actions in public is often counterproductive.

Question 6: Board development

What should the role of the executive director be at a board meeting?

Reply: The executive director should meet with the board chair a few weeks before the board meeting to discuss the agenda. The ED should brief the board chair on all items on the agenda. The ED's written report should be in the packet sent in advance of the meeting to all board members.

At the meeting, the ED should sit next to the board chair who leads the meeting. Because the board chair has been briefed on all major items, when a question arises, the board chair can usually answer it. If necessary, the chair will call on the ED for answers to specific questions.

The ED's report will be an agenda item. The ED will discuss items occurring since sending the report to the board members and will then ask if there are any questions. As a general rule of thumb, the ED should not speak for more than 10 percent of the time at a board meeting.

Qustion 7: Fundraising

What steps should I take to raise funds for my agency by conducting a phone-a-thon?

Reply: A phone-a-thon is an effective way of raising money. I volunteered to chair a phone-a-thon for my university. The most money raised by previous phone-a-thons was about $7,500. When I suggested that we use students as callers, members of the planning committee were less than enthusiastic, but they told me to go ahead and see what would happen.

I asked for a meeting with groups of students, including fraternity members, non-fraternity members, campus dwellers, and commuters. I asked what was the one item the students wanted, and after some discussion it was reported back to me that they wanted a gigantic, state-of-the-art television set. I said I would buy them the television if they would supply me with at least 50 students who would make phone calls for at least one night of the eight nights we were making calls.

Attending a one-hour training session was a prerequisite for any student agreeing to make calls. The training session included the distribution and review of the information about the new library, the project for which the contributions were going to be used. It included a discussion of techniques to use when making the calls. Every student had an opportunity to role-play. They played the role of the caller, and I played the role of the alumnus being called.

As part of the orientation, the students were told about the incentives. They included:

- Purchase of the big-screen TV for the student lounge.

- Unlimited pizza and sodas each of the eight evenings we were making calls.

- A $100 U.S. Savings Bond for the fraternity raising the most money.

- A $100 U.S. Savings Bond for the individual raising the most money.

- A $50 U.S. Savings Bond for any student raising more than $1,000.

Every student signed up to make phone calls a minimum of one of the eight nights. Calls were made between 7 p.m. and 9 p.m., Monday through Thursday, for two weeks. Students were told that they could make calls for as many nights as they wished. All calls were made to alumni by students who were sitting in the same large room. Students were given cards for each call, which included:

- Name, address, phone number, degree, and graduating class of alumnus.

- Amount of contributions to the university in previous phoneathons or other fundraising campaigns.

- Any other information about the alumnus supplied by the alumni office (for instance, their occupation, and any accomplishments, either before or after graduation).

Each time a pledge of $100 or more was made, I would ring a bell and write both the amount of the pledge and the student's name on a blackboard. I would also replenish the pizzas and sodas and provide additional refreshments as needed.

The bottom line was that after all expenses—TV purchase, cash prizes, and refreshments—the phone-a-thon raised more then $25,000 for the new library. This fundraiser was a big success.

Question 8: Fundraising

Should board and staff members be required to contribute to an agency's annual fundraising campaign, or buy tickets to an agency's special event?

Reply: Certainly. It is extremely helpful in any community campaign to announce that every board and staff member has contributed. There should not be a required contribution level, however. Everyone should contribute what they can afford. No announcement should be made of any gift amount or gift range without the express permission of the donor.

In many cases, particular board and staff members should receive complimentary tickets to special events. For example, if the tickets cost $100 a person for an agency fundraiser, complimentary tickets should be given to board and staff members who otherwise could not afford to attend.

Question 9: Grant writing

I have never written a grant before. I came to this workshop because I have received a Request for Proposal and am preparing to reply. How long should it take to write the proposal?

Reply: It depends. Writing a proposal might take as little as a half day if you work in a "functional agency," and at least three or four years if you work in a "nonfunctional agency." If you have previously conducted an assessment of the need of the citizens your agency serves, it will take you about an hour to review that assessment and fine-tune it for inclusion in the proposal you are writing. If you have never conducted a formal study of the needs of the citizens you serve, it might take a year to complete the needs assessment.

Next, you will answer the question in the RFP relating to the objectives of the proposal. If your agency has developed an excellent strategic plan, you might spend about an hour selecting two or three meaningful and measurable objectives from the plan to include in your proposal. If your agency has not developed a current strategic plan with meaningful and measurable objectives, it will take you at least a year to complete one.

If your agency has a set of current job descriptions, you just need to select which ones to include in the proposal you are writing. This might take you about a half hour.

If you have no job descriptions, you need to begin the process of developing them. This might take about three months.

If your agency has an evaluation process, answering the question in the RFP regarding evaluation will not take you more than a half an hour. If your agency does not have an evaluation process, it could take about six months to develop and implement one.

Finally, if your agency has a system whereby you know exactly how much it costs for every item to be purchased with agency funds, you can develop a budget for the program you are writing inside of an hour. However, if you don't have a clue how much items cost, developing an acceptable and auditable system might take at least six months.

Because every proposal you ever write will have the same basic sections, start now to develop them. Develop the "generic" grant. Then when a particular proposal must be written, you can draft it in a half a day.

Question 10: Grant management

What steps should we take after we receive a notice that our grant has been funded? Will the funding source send us a complete list of rules we will be expected to follow?

Reply: You will often be sent a contract by the funding source. You will be asked to sign the contract and return it. Make sure you read the terms of the contract carefully. Many times, you are so excited to receive the funds that you will sign the contract without even reading it. Don't do it!

Make sure to read the contract carefully. If there is a provision in the contract with which you don't agree, contact a representative of the funding source and ask that it be changed. If there is a provision you don't understand, you might check with your attorney or ask the funding source for more information.

If you are awarded fewer funds than you requested, make sure you change the budget and the objectives before signing the contract. Otherwise, you will be expected to meet the original objectives without the funds you need.

Many times, the funding source will require you to comply with specific laws in implementing the grant. Make sure you are fully aware of these laws before signing the contract.

If there are areas in which you have not received procedures, ask for them. Emphasize that you want to know all the rules you will be expected to follow. You want to avoid being criticized for not following rules you never knew existed.

If you must follow a rule that will create a difficult situation for you, ask for a meeting with the funding source right away and explain your problem. For example, many funding sources will only reimburse you for expenditures after you have made them. This means you must pay an employee performing tasks under a grant from your own funds, and then wait to be reimbursed by the funding source. If your agency does not have funds to pay the employee, ask the funding source what to do. If you must borrow from a bank to pay the employee, who is going to cover the cost of the loan? Recommend that the funding source provide you with the funds to make approved expenditures before the expenditures are made.

Before the computer age, many funding sources required you to place money from their grant in a separate account and have different checkbooks for different grants. Yet, even though this is an unnecessary rule today, many agencies still require this. If the funding source still has this rule, ask for it to be waived.

Many funding sources require you to return any interest earned to the funding source. If the interest earned is minimal or if it would be difficult to calculate the amount of interest generated by each grant, ask if you can keep any interest earned if you use it for the purpose of the grant.

Question 11: Strategic planning

What should the time period be for a strategic plan?

Reply: It depends. It should be for as long a period as it is reasonable to plan in advance. If the community and the services are relatively stable, it may be possible to plan for five years or more. In a volatile agency, however, where the agency has control of few of the variables, even planning for two years in advance may be impossible.

Question 12: Supervision

How should a supervisor handle an employee who is unpleasant?

Reply: The supervisor should document the specific unpleasant behavior. He or she should then set up a private, uninterrupted meeting with the employee. The employee should not be told that they are unpleasant, but that certain words they used, or actions they took, interfered with the agency's mission of providing excellent service to the community. The employee should then be given examples of ways to handle similar situations that arise in the future.

Question 13: Supervision

You said that I should delegate tasks assigned to our unit based on factors including the capabilities of the workers and my trust in the staff. Wouldn't that mean the same worker would receive all of the "special assignments?"

Reply: Excellent question. Let's say you are supervising three individuals in a nonprofit agency. You have been given an important assignment by the board of directors and must decide to whom to delegate it. If the nonprofit is at all typical, if you have three employees reporting to you, one will be *excellent*, one will be *average*, and one will be *terrible*. What would you do? Of course, you would assign the task to the *excellent* worker. This is the worker who would complete the assignment in a competent and timely manner.

The next day, you are given another important assignment to delegate. What would you do as an effective manager? Of course, you would assign it again to the *excellent* worker. After making this same responsible decision several more times, what would happen? The excellent worker eventually would get burned out and would realize that he or she was receiving significant amounts of extra work for no extra pay. Eventually, the worker would resent being given the additional assignments and would act in a dysfunctional manner.

Would the average worker step up to the plate and volunteer to perform the new additional work with no additional pay? Would he ask to be sent to additional training programs to obtain the skills so that he could be assigned the additional work?

Of course not. Indeed, he would try as hard as possible to avoid getting the new assignments. If he had the opportunity to learn new skills, he would avoid doing this because he is average, not stupid. If he acquired new skills, he would be given new assignments at no additional pay so he would act in a dysfunctional manner in order not to receive the new assignment.

Would the terrible worker volunteer for the new tasks? Of course not. Indeed, what choice words would the terrible worker use to describe the excellent worker? Words like "idiot," "brownnoser," and other words that cannot be repeated in a general circulation book. The worker might actively sabotage the operation and do everything possible so that the new work would not be done well or at all.

So you, as the effective manager, would have made the sensible decision and you would now find yourself in a difficult situation. What should you do? Perhaps the first new assignment should be given to the excellent worker.

But then assign the next one to the terrible worker. If he or she refuses to accept the assignment, or does not complete it in a timely or effective manner, begin disciplinary procedures and then after that begin procedures to fire the terrible worker. At some point, a manager cannot be effective if any of his workers is not effective. Disciplinary and firing procedures are established to rid your unit of unproductive workers.

Question 14: Supervision

How can I get my work done when the individuals I supervise are always coming to my office to ask me questions? However, if I don't let them ask me questions, I won't be doing my job as supervisor.

Reply: Many supervisors believe that a trait of a good supervisor is to have an open door policy and to invite their workers to come to their offices with any type of problem. This policy will lead to a great deal of wasted time on behalf of both the supervisor and the worker. Instead, the supervisor should say, come see me when the following conditions are met:

- You are seeing me about a problem I would be willing to help you solve. For example, if is a personal problem totally unrelated to the office, don't share it with me. If it is a problem you should be solving all by yourself, don't discuss it with me.

- Before you come see me about a problem, find out as many facts as you can on your own. It is not a good use of time to present a problem to me when you only know half the facts.

♦   When you see me, be prepared to make a recommendation as to what you would do next if you were in my position. Give me pros and cons related to different courses of action.

Question 15: Supervision

Does everyone have to have a supervisor? My agency works to reduce sexual harassment of women. Rather than the traditional "hierarchical method" of having one individual supervise several others, the women in my agency work in "sisterhood" fashion with full discussions of issues and no one is the supervisor.

Reply: I asked the woman who posed this question who made the decisions if there were a conflict among the women in the unit that they could not resolve. She said that she did. I said "Let's call *you* the supervisor." I asked her which staff member reported on the staff's activities to the board and she said that she did. So I said, "You have made my point. You definitely are the supervisor."

Every executive director should have a supervisor. In many organizations, the executive director is not properly supervised. I reviewed the organization of one nonprofit and observed that the executive director received no supervision at all. When I pointed this out at a board meeting, board members told me the board chair was supposed to supervise the executive director. So I met with the board chair. She said she didn't think she should be supervising the executive director because she was "just a volunteer," and the ED was an expert in his field.

I asked her to tell me about her work experiences. She explained that she was the supervisor at a department store. I asked her to list her supervisory duties in the department store so we could determine which ones were applicable to her responsibilities as supervisor of the executive director. This was an important exercise. She then began to meet with the executive director on a regular basis to review his schedule and to inform him of items the board needed for the next board meeting. The ED would get advice from the board chair on numerous items before making a decision. They would discuss which specific issues needed board approval and which did not.

After a few weeks, they made a list of which supervisory responsibilities the board chair would undertake. Both the board chair and the executive director felt comfortable in these new roles.

In another situation, I was evaluating a daycare program that included 12 daycare centers. Each center had a similar structure with a head teacher, a number of other teachers and several aides. When I asked the agency's executive director who provided supervision at each center, he said that the head teacher did. However, when I reviewed the decisions that were made at each center, it was clear that the head teacher did not provide supervision.

Training, hiring, scheduling, disciplining, firing, and many similar duties were undertaken by different individuals in the central office. The head teacher just was a teacher who had more experience than the other teachers at each center and was paid a little more. For the most part, the head teacher's duties were no different than those of the other teachers. Staff members at each center were provided with limited or no supervision, or they received supervision from several different people in the central office. So one of the tasks I undertook was to recommend a workable supervisory system.

The most egregious example of little or no supervision was presented early in my career when I was hired as an administrator of an agency with more than 500 employees. A major personnel consulting firm had just completed a study of the agency and one of its findings was that "more than 60 percent of the employees could not identify their supervisor correctly." For example, when asked to list the name of their supervisor, many individuals named the individual in the central personnel office who approved their leave requests. Indeed, the main reason most individuals could not name their supervisor was that they received little or no supervision.

One last story: I was leading an all-day workshop on supervisory techniques for county employees. At 2 p.m., three of the attendees said they had to leave. When I asked why, they said they were supervisors at the laundry at the county nursing home and they had to be present at 3 p.m. when the shift changed. I asked whether they had benefited from the workshop and they said they had. But one said, "Mr. Sand, the one thing you emphasized that we can't do is when you said a supervisor can tell the workers what they should be doing. We can't do that." I told them that I felt this was an essential element of supervision and asked why they couldn't do that. One of the other workers said, "Mr. Sand, when we go back to the home, if we would tell the workers what to do, they would not listen and would probably throw us into the laundry vats." The other laundry "supervisors" shook their heads in agreement. I decided not to volunteer to help solve this problem.

Question 16: Supervision

Am I allowed to stop unpleasant conduct by the individuals I supervise such as racist humor, sexual harassment, and gossip? What if these individuals are doing their work appropriately?

Reply: I feel strongly that the answer to this question is definitely "yes." My reasoning is that an employee cannot be doing work appropriately if engaged in conduct that is illegal or offensive. In addition, when engaged in this conduct, an employee invariably stops other employees from performing their duties in an effective manner.

The first step you should take as a manager is to meet with those whom you supervise to make sure they know the difference between appropriate and inappropriate conduct. If an employee wishes to tell a joke that involves making fun of individuals in a particular ethnic group, for example, should they be permitted to tell it at work? One simple test is whether they would tell the joke if a member of the group being made fun of were in the room.

Similarly, to understand what constitutes sexual harassment does not require a law degree. When thinking about making a particular statement to a female employee, for example, think whether you would be upset if an individual made that same comment to your mother or wife. If so, the comment should be forbidden in the workplace.

The biblical "golden rule" is a good rule to apply when determining whether certain speech is "gossip," and should not be made in the workplace. If you would be upset if an individual made a particular comment about you, you should not make it to a fellow employee.

Another principle is when you have indicated as a manager that particular speech is unacceptable in the workplace, stop it every time it occurs. Do not allow one individual to engage in inappropriate conduct and then stop another from engaging in the same conduct.

Question 17: Organizational excellence

What steps should I take to make my organization excellent?

Reply: That is an excellent question because all nonprofits should strive to be excellent. The best answer I can give is to refer you to a national organization whose mission is to provide specific answers to this question: the Standards for Excellence Institute.

Take a look at the 56 Standards for Excellence provided by this group, which are divided into areas such as mission, board development, finances, personnel, fundraising, and public policy. You can view these standards by visiting *www.standardsforexcellence.org*, and learn what your state is doing in this important area.

Another step your organization can take is to make certain the documents referred to in this book are updated frequently and are referred to often by board and staff members as guides for decision-making. They include:

- bylaws.

- needs assessment.

- strategic plan.

- ◆   personnel evaluation plan.

- ◆   program evaluation plan.

- ◆   program budgeting system.

In my experience, every excellent nonprofit has most or all of these six documents, and refers to them on a regular basis.

Index

213

C

About the Author

Michael A. Sand is the founder of Sand Associates, a nationwide management consulting firm based in Harrisburg, Pennsylvania. He received his undergraduate and law degrees from the University of Pennsylvania and a Masters Degree in Public Administration from Penn State University. In 1966, he began his career as a staff member in the Philadelphia and Montgomery County (PA) anti-poverty programs. Then, he served as deputy director of the Pennsylvania Bureau of Consumer Protection, and Administrator of the Law Bureau of the Pennsylvania Public Utility Commission. He was named the first executive director of the Community Action Association of Pennsylvania.

Since the formation of Sand Associates in 1979, Mike has led workshops throughout the country in each of the nine topics corresponding to the chapters in this book. He has led more than 1000 workshops at conferences and for individual agencies and nonprofit associations, and has taught courses at several universities. In addition, he has helped nonprofits to develop strategic plans, raise funds, strengthen boards, write grants, recruit volunteers, evaluate programs, and improve many other aspects of nonprofit management. Sand's firm includes more than 100 associates with expertise in all aspects of nonprofit management.